HOW TO INCREASE
PROFITS
WITH
COST
MANAGEMENT

HOW TO INCREASE PROFITS WITH COST MANAGEMENT

By

CARLTON D. RICHARDSON, C.P.A.

A COMPREHENSIVE GUIDE TO IMPROVING
PROFITS BY AVOIDING, PREVENTING,
AND ELIMINATING UNNECESSARY COSTS

88881

DUQUESNE PUBLISHING COMPANY
Post Office Box 85   Moorestown, N.J. 08057

SPECIAL LIMITED
LIBRARY EDITION

First Edition

Second Printing, 1979

Copyright © 1978 by Carlton D. Richardson

All Rights Reserved

Library of Congress Catalog Card No. 77-91605

International Standard Book Number 0-89653-011-6

Manufactured in the United States of America

Harlo Press, 50 Victor Avenue, Detroit, Michigan 48203

To Lois,
for her unfailing help and encouragement,
especially with this book.

An executive cannot gradually dismiss details. Business is made up of details and I notice that the chief executive who dismisses them is quite likely to dismiss his business.

Success is the sum of detail. It might perhaps be pleasing to imagine oneself beyond detail and engaged only in great things, but as I have often observed, if one attends only to great things and lets the little things pass the great things become little; that is, the business shrinks.

It is not possible for an executive to hold himself aloof from anything. No business, no matter what its size, can be called safe until it has been forced to learn economy and rigidly to measure values of men and materials.

—Harvey S. Firestone

CONTENTS

1. INTRODUCTION   15

   Cost Reduction vs. Cost Management, 15; How to Get the Most Out of This Book, 17

2. MANAGER ATTITUDES ABOUT COSTS   21

   Why Costs Are Important, 21; Why Costs Get Out of Control, 24; The Cost Conscious Attitude, 27; Developing a Cost Conscious Attitude, 29; The Cost Conscious Manager, 32

3. THE SIX-STEP COST MANAGEMENT APPROACH   35

   Cost Avoidance, 36; Cost Prevention, 37; Cost Elimination, 38; Cost Reduction, 39; Cost Management, 40; The Six Simple Steps, 41; Developing Your Cost Management Abilities, 42; Opening Your Mind to Cost Improvement Ideas, 43; Cultivating a Cost Improvement Atmosphere, 43; Review of Step One, 44

4. ANALYZING AND UNDERSTANDING YOUR OPERATIONS   47

   Understanding Your Operations, 48; The Cost Management Review, 49; The Organization Review, 50; The XYZ Company, 51; Formal vs. Implied Objectives, 54; The Systems Review, 55; The Function Review, 57; The Staffing Review, 58; Staffing Review Example, 59; The

9

XYZ Company Operations Improvement Program Example, 61; The Program Review, 67; Summary, 68

5. EVALUATING YOUR OPERATIONS   71

What Are Costs?, 71; What Is Cost Improvement?, 72; Condition Your Thinking, 72; Three Questions to Ask About Every Function, 73; An Overall View of the Evaluation Process, 74; Dividing Activities into Evaluation Categories, 75; Question Everything, 76; Challenge Every Activity, 78; General Questions to Ask When You Evaluate Your Operations, 79

6. MANAGING ASSETS
   FOR PROFIT IMPROVEMENT   99

Cash, 99; Accounts Receivable, 102; Inventories, 105; Other Current Assets, 109; Fixed Assets, 109; Summary, 111

7. EVALUATING PRODUCT COSTS   113

Standard Cost Systems, 114; Material, 118; A Team Approach for Managing Material Costs, 119; Direct Labor, 120; A Simplified Approach for Measuring Direct Labor Productivity, 121; Let Labor Work Smarter Not Harder, 122; Manufacturing Overhead, 123; General Questions to Ask About Manufacturing Operations, 125; Specific Questions About Manufacturing Operations, 135; Looking at Specific Overhead Costs, 138; Summary, 145

8. MANAGING COMMON OFFICE COSTS   147

Telephones, 147; The Basic Equipment Charge, 148; Long Distance and Message Unit Charges, 151; Wide Area Telecommunications Service (WATS), 154; Foreign Exchange Service, 156; Getting Assistance to Evaluate Your Telephone Costs, 156; Mailing and Postage Costs, 157; Mail Room Operations, 159; Office Supplies and Forms Costs, 160; Establishing a Forms Control Program, 163; Other Common Office Costs, 167

9. DEVELOPING COST
   IMPROVEMENT IDEAS   171

   The Time for Developing Cost Improvement Ideas, 172;
   Your Place for Developing Ideas, 173; Ways to Develop
   Ideas, 174; Idea-starter Words, 181; Developing Your
   Own Methods, 183; Summary, 183

10. STEPS FIVE AND SIX   185

11. PARTING WORDS   189

HOW TO INCREASE
PROFITS
WITH
COST
MANAGEMENT

1 INTRODUCTION

Cost reduction is relatively easy. A few strokes of the pen to prepare the appropriate memo and the order is given to eliminate a department, close a factory, or layoff 10% of the salaried employees. Nothing to it.

Cost Management is more difficult. It takes understanding, innovation, and action. Understanding to know where and why costs are being incurred, innovation to develop ideas on how to prevent and eliminate them, and action to implement those improvement ideas.

Too many managers think in terms of cost reduction rather than cost management. They forget that it's as important to be ready for tomorrow as it is to make today look good. They forget too that managing costs is a basic responsibility of every operating manager.

In theory this management responsibility sounds simple. Most managers would not deny that they must manage costs as well as people, but in actual practice they often avoid this basic responsibility. They simply fail to meet their cost management responsibility with the same directness that they attack the more technical aspects of their particular management field.

Most managers were promoted to their present position because they were proficient in a particular technical field of endeavor. Many have never been trained in the various techniques of analyzing and evaluating costs. As a result, more businesses fail from lack of understanding and control of costs than from lack of technical knowledge and ability.

I believe that lack of training in Cost Management Techniques is the major reason why so many managers fail to approach this management responsibility with the same zeal they show for developing new products, increasing sales, or planning expansions of the business.

Avoiding, preventing and eliminating costs is considered a negative attitude by many of today's expansion minded executives. It could mean the elimination of product lines, the scaling down of future plans, and even the lowering of sales volumes in order to improve the bottom line profit picture.

This book is about managing costs, i.e., avoiding, preventing, and eliminating unnecessary costs in order to keep them at that reasonable minimum level needed to sustain an adequate level of profits. It is intended for all managers from the shop floor foreman to the president of a company who are genuinely interested in increasing the profitability of their operations.

Initial focus is on the development of a cost conscious attitude. Later chapters discuss what costs are, how they can be identified and compared with the benefits or non-benefits they produce, and point out the action needed to make the most of every dollar. Other chapters discuss evaluation of operations, development of improvements, and other specific cost areas.

Many books about cost reduction and profit improvement tend in varying degrees to stress accounting techniques or procedures involved. At the other extreme are behavioral studies dealing with the psychological, emotional, or physical impact that cost reduction campaigns have on personnel. The following pages are meant to fill the gap between these two extremes and to put in one handbook a simple, understandable approach for use by managers on a practical day-to-day basis.

The book outlines a six-step management approach for eliminating unnecessary costs. Then it explores in greater depth specific cost areas and functions that are found in most companies. It utilizes the principle that it is more important for a manager to know how to ask the right questions about his operations, than to know *all* of the answers.

There are hundreds of cost saving and profit improvement ideas in the form of questions for the manager to ask about his operations. The questions posed have been used effectively by other operating managers to analyze and improve their operations. They have met the test of practical application by the supervisors, managers and executives of many diversified companies. They have been reorganized and edited for publication in this convenient book form to provide operating managers with a manual for profit improvement.

Using the questions and techniques discussed in the following chapters you can objectively examine a department's or company's current operations, appraise the results, and then develop new or revised programs which will prevent or eliminate costs to achieve greater profitability.

It is hoped that this book will not only give managers a better understanding of costs, but will also be of long-term value in developing a cost conscious attitude among their subordinates.

Newly made managers will find this book helpful in developing cost effective methods for their own responsibilities and a source of ideas for their effective participation as a member of the management team. Experienced executives will find it valuable in reappraising overall operations and upgrading their skills in evaluating the cost effectiveness of their subordinate managers.

How to Get the Most Out of This Book
This book is intended for men and women who seriously want to do something about unnecessary costs to assure

the financial success of their company and themselves. Its purpose is to be of constructive help. Your alert and active participation is absolutely essential to gain the most from these pages. It is not a general discussion about costs but rather a step-by-step approach to help you eliminate costs which obstruct the true profit potential of your operations.

Make this a working book, not just a reading book. Keep a note pad and pencil handy to jot down any notes, questions or ideas which come to mind as you read each chapter. Ask yourself, "How can I apply this to my operations or department?" Pretend you are attending a workshop seminar where you expect to hear interesting and stimulating cost improvement ideas to take back to your job.

When you come to the various example questions, answer them if they apply to your area of responsibility. Write out your answers. You may be surprised how much more precise you can make an answer once you've seen it on paper. If you don't want to write them down, try saying them aloud into a tape recorder or dictation machine. If you verbalize your answers, on paper or aloud, they will be more real and more precise.

Make a note of anything covered in this book that you believe may be applicable to your operations. It doesn't matter whether you agree with my view, the important thing is to call attention to ideas you feel should be considered in more detail. As you read there may be questions or ideas that you think of other than the examples listed. As you think of them, make notes so you can consider them later. When you've finished the book, go back and review those ideas; think about them until you're satisfied that each idea noted either can be applied to improve your operations, or must be discarded.

Then collect the remaining notes and prepare a definite plan for implementing the cost improvement ideas you have discovered. This book has not served its purpose unless it stimulates, inspires and specifically helps you to develop concrete ideas which will improve the cost effectiveness of your operations.

Although an idea may not be applicable today, it may be sometime in the future when you change jobs or get promoted. A quick reference back to this book will refresh you on the details.

2 MANAGER ATTITUDES ABOUT COSTS

The manager today is faced with increasingly complex problems. Consumers, employees, and government demand greater product reliability and safety, higher salaries and wages, and more stringent environmental pollution standards. Concurrently these same groups demand lower prices, shorter working hours, and more detail government reporting. While managers grope to come up with solutions to these conflicting demands, the stockholders of business and industry are insisting on greater profitability, growth and dividends. More than ever before there is a premium being placed on a manager's ability to reduce costs and improve profits.

This book is designed to make a manager's life more livable by providing him not only with an approach to understanding the costs and profitability of his operations, but with methods for identifying waste or costs which do not contribute to profits.

Why Costs Are Important
Sometime ago, I was discussing the possibility of investing in an apartment building with a real estate agent. "There are three important rules to remember when buying real estate," he said.

"What are they?" I asked, anxious to learn the secrets he had to offer.

"Location, location, location," he replied.

At the time I thought he was being overly emphatic about one of the many things to consider when investing in real estate; but later, after I had bought and sold several properties, I realized he had given me sound advice. The better locations commanded a higher price, were easier to finance, easier to rent, easier to sell when that time came, and much more profitable in the long run.

There are also three important rules to make profits soar. Cost, cost, and cost. Management's ability to avoid, prevent, and eliminate costs usually means the difference between success or failure.

Customers buy from one company rather than another because there is at least *one* thing that company offers which their competitors do not. It may be price, quality, style, service, location, or any of a dozen other factors. Whatever it is, it brings orders to their door. However, over a period of time the competition will identify that unique factor and develop ways to improve on it. Unless costs have been kept at a reasonable minimum, profits soon become losses in the resulting competitive market.

Despite all that has been written and said about the aims and goals of business, the first objective of any business is to make a profit. Without profits a business will fail. Effective management of costs will not only maintain or improve current profit levels, but also strengthen the Company's competitive position in future markets.

Not all businessmen agree with the importance of costs. Ask a salesman about improving profits and he will tell you that his most important activity is *sales*. Nothing happens until the sale is made. However, sales will not increase profits if the sales price isn't enough to cover all operating costs; such as, the cost of the product, the cost of shipping, billing and collecting receivables, the cost of carrying appropriate inventories, etc.

Ask the Research and Development manager how to

improve profits and he will tell you, "By producing a better product." However, that better product has to be designed and produced at a price the customers are willing to pay.

Ask the Industrial Relations manager and he will tell you the most important element to improve profits is, "Hiring and training good people. Our most important resource is our employees." But, those employees represent cost in terms of salaries, fringes and office or plant space.

Ask the Manufacturing manager how to improve profits and he will tell you, "Modernize the plant equipment to make it more efficient." But, new equipment increases capital costs, which may not be warranted.

One could go on and relate the typical answer each manager gives when asked for profit improvement ideas. However, I think we all see that managing costs is of utmost importance in all answers. In fact, the five M's of business—Men, Money, Machines, Materials, and Minutes —all result in the generation of costs. The same is true in our personal lives. We must effectively manage costs at home in order to get those things we want—shelter, food, clothing, transportation, entertainment, etc.—within the limits of our income. Thus, our financial success at home or in business is directly related to our skill in the management of costs.

Regardless of whether your field of management is a small department or a whole company, knowing how to eliminate or prevent costs can mean the difference between success and failure. Often, how well you manage the daily task of getting the most out of a dollar determines the outcome of a promotion, a raise you have been waiting for, or whether you exceed your job objectives.

The rewards of good cost management can be considerable or they can be meager. The cost conscious manager who owns his own business could end up a millionaire, the manager of a successful operation in a company could get promoted, the housewife who applies cost management in the home could salt away a tidy bank account. On the other hand, a manager may be so surrounded by "budgetpadders" that his efforts go unrecognized or the housewife's husband gambles away her savings. There is always, however, the pleasure of achievement, and the cost effective manager can measure his achievement in terms of dollars and cents.

It is one thing to suggest that cost management can be useful, profitable and exciting, but quite another thing to suggest that it can be applied directly to your particular operating situation. So before we discuss specific cost management techniques, let's first explore why costs get out of control.

Why Costs Get Out of Control

Ask any manager about his operations and sometime during the conversation he will insist that costs are a primary concern to him and to his management team. Probe him a little about his ongoing programs to manage daily costs and the discussion will begin to get vague. Probe deeper about the specific cost of his various departments or a specific cost item such as telephone or office supplies. If he is honest, he will usually admit it has been a long time since he really paid much attention to the operations on such a detailed basis. He will explain that he has been busy with expansion plans, or market conditions, or overall planning, and has left the managing of day-to-day costs with the managers who report to him.

Of course his managers or supervisors are taking their leadership from him. Since his concern is with the new expansion plans, then that is where they are spending their time and energy, because they want to be in a position to give their boss the answers when he discusses the latest project. And so it goes all the way down the pyramid until it reaches the clerks at the bottom. The clerk at the bottom of the pyramid isn't thinking about the cost of operations because he only sees a small part of the operations. Besides, he is too busy getting all the bills paid to worry about the fact that the cost of telephones is twice as much as last year. He probably doesn't even know that the actual volume only increased 10% over last year. And so it goes from department to department, each concentrating on his particular specialty.

With inflation, costs are bound to increase. It's a way of life. As costs creep up, waste creeps in, and even though sales increase 10%, profits go up only 7 to 8 percent. As long as profits in total are higher, management carelessly adjusts to a why-worry-about-it attitude.

Then a swing in the economic cycle occurs and the business hits what we call "tough times." Top management begins to realize there is a problem and shifts its attention to a more detailed look at operations. After all, there are no expansion plans to concentrate on now. The managers are job oriented to a growing operation and a growing economy. Their first reaction to economic adversity is to increase sales, to get the volume up, cover the fixed overhead at the plant, although they may have only a vague notion what that is. Special prices are given to customers to spur sales and volumes are maintained—for awhile. However, costs continue to increase. With decreasing margins to support these increased costs the inevitable losses are fast to follow.

Top management now begins to be really concerned. The stockholders are putting on the pressure. There is talk of change in some top positions. They begin their scramble to understand the situation and look for massive changes which will plug the holes in the sinking ship.

The managers are forced to shift from their former expansion minded style to a foreign mode of economy operation. To them cost management is a random problem forced on them by the change in the economy or the environment of their particular industry. Suddenly their superiors are asking why operations are so costly and demanding cost justification for projects which had always been accepted at face value.

Anyone who has experienced the sinking of his company and/or the economy will never forget it. It is both painful and frustrating. Good programs are junked. Valuable personnel are eliminated because staff must be reduced. Many of the better employees leave by choice rather than wait for the ax to fall. The marginal employees, those who would have difficulty finding other employment, stay on as long as possible. Sometimes these marginal or less desirable employees survive the crisis and it is they who are left to rebuild the company.

Whole operations are cut back, plants are closed to eliminate or slow down the losses, and everyone knows the road to recovery afterwards will be a long one. While the technically competent, enthusiastic employees who made the company great (the very blood of the organization) flow out of it, top executives mutter about over-expansion, collapsing markets or mismanagement of the economy by the government.

Does the foregoing sound familiar? If it doesn't, then your company has been extremely lucky. If it hasn't happened to your company, it will, unless there is a very strong cost management program to prevent it.

Companies often fail to keep cost management as a basic part of their management program. Sure, they have suggestion programs, value analysis departments, and work simplification efforts, but the effect of over-expansion, over-organization, and neglect of costs cannot be stopped by such routine staff efforts. To keep a company healthy and flexible so that it can cope with the inevitable economic fluctuations, requires an approach to cost management which demands constant management attention. There must be a program against which managers' performance can be measured and one which will motivate innovation and creativity.

Costs get out of control because *management does not have a consistent attitude toward cost management.* They do not reward cost management achievements equitably, and in many cases the more experienced "budget padder" will survive where the honest cost conscious manager will be extremely frustrated until he learns to play the game.

Effective cost management requires breaking away

from the old, self-perpetuating attitudes and generating new ways of looking at your operations. It requires the development of a *cost conscious attitude*. Only when this attitude has been acquired can cost management techniques be practiced and used as a skill which improves with experience.

This type of attitude is not limited to the business enterprise alone, but is a practical need of everyone both at home and on the job.

The Cost Conscious Attitude

Many managers display one of three attitudes toward cutting costs; i.e., they dismiss the problem as being someone else's job, they set unrealistic goals to impress higher management without any programs to accomplish such goals, or, they scarcely think about costs at all.

We will discuss the first two attitudes in greater detail later on but first, let's examine the third most common and most dangerous attitude; not worrying about costs at all.

Many managers attained their present position because of their technical expertise in some particular field. They were good salesmen, engineers, or production specialists, and, as a result, were promoted to managerial positions. Suddenly their ability to close the big sale, improve the product performance, or handle day-to-day labor problems is not important in their new responsibilities. Higher management now expects them to give more attention to profits. Many enter this new stage in their career with little or no understanding of how to keep costs in line with benefits to be derived from each expenditure.

Managers on the job for some period of time are forced to recognize the importance of costs, but often fail to accept their responsibility for cost management by convincing themselves that it is of lesser importance than their daily functions. They consciously or subconsciously abdicate cost control responsibilities to the Controller, General Manager, or anyone else who seems a likely candidate for the job. They then concentrate their attention on the "today" problems in their department. They go through the motions annually of preparing budgets and forecasts; dutifully include fat cushions to provide for all possible contingencies, and studiously develop standard reasons why budget overruns are someone else's responsibility or beyond their control.

Setting totally unrealistic goals is usually demonstrated by the manager who finds himself under heavy pressure from top management to improve operations. Rather than planning specifically and implementing new approaches to achieve those goals which would accomplish the improvements requested, he takes the "easy way out" by projecting unrealistically higher sales and lower costs. His profit plans are what he *hopes* for, not what he really *expects* will happen. Often because higher management really likes to hear good news, they accept the optimistic plans with only limited evaluation. This approach gets the manager through the critical budget preparation period, but does not actually discharge his responsibility for managing his costs.

When actual results are compared to his optimistic forecast, this kind of manager is quick to blame his poor showing on someone else or a change in conditions. Thus consciously or subconsciously he assumes that cutting costs is simply someone else's job.

Does the above sound exaggerated? It isn't. Experience over the years has shown many individual managers whose attitudes parallel those outlined. If a manager discounts the value of budget comparisons during the first year that budget techniques are introduced, it is understandable. There is a period of adjustment until managers develop cost effective approaches. However, after the second or third year, the same old excuses sound like "broken records."

I have never fully understood the mental block that some managers have in the area of cost management, especially anyone proficient enough to attain the job of being a manager in the first place. Development of a cost conscious attitude is easily achieved and can only improve a manager's potential both to the company and to himself.

Developing a Cost Conscious Attitude
What is a cost conscious attitude? How can we develop one if we don't feel that way now? Generally speaking, being cost conscious is a combination of many personal attributes. Most of us possess many of them already and with self-discipline we can strengthen the others. The chart on the next page lists some of them and as you review it, I am sure you will think of others.

THE COST CONSCIOUS ATTITUDE

A lert   — Always looking for profit opportunities.

C urious   — A constant spirit of inquiry.
O bjective   — Takes the unbiased viewpoint.
S elective   — Able to choose the major opportunity.
T houghtful   — Thinks through the situation.

C oncentration   — Penetrates the problem in depth.
O pen-minded   — Willing to listen to all suggestions.
N oting   — Makes notes of every possible solution.
S pecific   — Picks the key to the problem.
C ommunicative   — Able to relate ideas to others.
I nterested   — Willing to dig below the surface.
O bservant   — Notices why things work the way they do.
U nderstanding   — Listens to others' points of view.
S ensitive   — Respects the needs of others.

A ware   — Understands the opportunities around him.
T actful   — Fills the needs of others' feelings.
T enacity   — Sees the problem to completion.
I nvolved   — Wants to be a part of the problem.
T horough   — Always gets all the facts.
U ndaunted   — Undiscouraged by the pitfalls encountered.
D etermination   — Does everything to assure success.
E nthusiasm   — Fully supports and stimulates others.

M otivated   — Self-moved without threat or reward.
E nergy   — Has the drive to do the job.
A pplication   — Applies his energy and effort.
N imble   — Has a quick, active mind for problem solving.
S ense   — Has a common sense approach.

P atient   — Gives enough time to develop details.
R ealistic   — Does not expect the impossible.
O ptimistic   — Combines enthusiasm and self-confidence.
F lexible   — Welcomes change and new conditions.
I nventive   — Tries to develop the unusual solution.
T eamworker   — Works productively with others.

The cost conscious manager is an individual who is always *alert* for profit improvement opportunities. He is *curious* enough to ask why things are done the way they are and *objective* enough to explore various alternatives in order to find better ways of doing things. He is a *thoughtful* individual, able to *concentrate* long enough on a problem to understand it in depth. After he has *selected* a major opportunity for improvement, he is *open-minded* enough to test his ideas by listening to other people's suggestions. He is an *interested, observant* person who *notes* every possible solution before trying to settle on a *specific* idea. He then is able to *communicate* his cost improvement ideas with *understanding* and *tact* in order to convince others of the benefits of the recommended change. *Aware* of the opportunities around him, he is also *sensitive* to the strong feelings others have about change. As an *involved* individual he is *thorough* in his analysis of the opportunity, *undaunted* by the pitfalls that are encountered and has the *determination* to follow each project to completion. His *tenacity* and *enthusiasm* stimulate those around him. Usually he is a *self-motivated, energetic* individual who is capable of *applying* himself and simple common *sense* to every possible cost improvement opportunity. Although he has a *nimble* mind, he is *patient* with others who do not grasp his concepts as quickly as he does and he is *realistic* in the goals he sets for himself and others. He is an *optimistic teamworker* who is *inventive* in developing cost improvement ideas. Although his primary drive is to reduce cost and improve profits, he is also *flexible* enough to recommend increased expenditures if they will provide adequate benefits to the company.

Now, no one possesses all thirty-three of these attributes in equal proportion, but most successful managers have a good many of them and are capable of developing the others.

Review the cost conscious attitude chart. How many of these attributes do you think you possess right now? Jot down each one on a sheet of paper and write "have" or "have not" opposite each. Be honest with yourself; remember, this is a self-analysis test. No one needs to know your score. Now, add up the "have's" and see how you scored without fooling yourself. If you scored twenty or more, you rate high and you're well started toward full development of a cost conscious attitude. If you scored fewer than twenty items, you had better go to work on yourself to develop those qualities. You know that you either possess these traits already or you're capable of developing them. It will pay you to keep rechecking the list and re-rating yourself periodically.

Push aside any negative feelings you have. Actively try to develop an open, alert awareness of the world around you. Being cost conscious is only fearful to those who know nothing about it. All you have to do is utilize those attributes you now have or are capable of developing and you will find that there are numerous cost improvement opportunities all around you. Just apply yourself fully to learning and practicing the cost improvement techniques in the following pages. You can make your own career more successful than you ever realized, if you develop and keep a cost conscious attitude.

The Cost Conscious Manager

By definition a manager plans, organizes, directs, and controls the activities of subordinates in order to achieve the objectives within his responsibility. The cost conscious manager accomplishes these same objectives but in a way that will make maximum use of the resources entrusted to him.

The manager's planning consists of defining his objectives and then developing programs, schedules, budgets, and forecasts to achieve those objectives. He then designs the organization structure, policies, procedures, and standards to implement his plans.

The cost conscious manager follows the same pattern, but he defines his objectives with costs and profitability in mind. His programs are action strategies which emphasize profitability while achieving the required objectives. His schedules not only show when individual activities will be started and completed, but also show the costs and the benefits of each activity. His budgets reflect detailed expected expenditures required to implement each program and his projections show the expected profitability from his anticipated results.

The cost conscious manager's organization is a deliberate design in number and kinds of positions, along with corresponding duties and responsibilities required to make maximum use of the people resources available to him. His policies are not only general guides for decision making, but emphasize cost and profitability guidelines. His procedures not only detail methods for carrying out the policies, but give cost and profitability benchmarks. His standards define cost levels for individual or group performance which is acceptable.

In directing and guiding his department the cost conscious manager, follows the same profitability theme. When staffing, training, supervising, delegating, motivating, counseling and coordinating he keeps cost emphasis in the forefront.

He staffs each required position, keeping in mind the relative cost of personnel and will refuse to fill positions with unqualified individuals simply because they have become excess in another department. When training, he teaches cost effectiveness as strongly as he does specific duties. His day-to-day supervision constantly emphasizes profitability. When delegating work, responsibilities, and authority, he attempts to make maximum use of his subordinates' abilities. He motivates by appealing to the needs of his subordinates while encouraging development of cost effective attitudes. His counseling with individual subordinates about their work and personal problems continues the profitability theme. His activities are coordinated and carried out in relation to their importance with a minimum of duplication and wasted effort.

The cost conscious manager controls his operation by

reviewing cost and profit results. He measures his progress toward his objectives in financial and other quantitative terms. He is constantly determining causes of significant deviations from his planned operations. He then takes steps to correct unfavorable trends or takes advantage of unusually favorable trends. He is therefore constantly improving his operations by developing more effective and/or economical methods.

Acquiring the cost conscious attitude discussed above is the first step of the Six-Step Cost Management Approach outlined in this book. Without this attitude it will be very difficult, if not impossible, to become an effective manager of your operation's costs.

3 THE SIX-STEP COST MANAGEMENT APPROACH

The managing of costs is a basic responsibility of the management function. A manager not only has the authority to manage the expenditures made by his department, but he also has the responsibility to plan, direct and control such costs in a manner which will generate the greatest return to the company.

Managers spend a great deal of time and effort trying to make operations more productive. Much less effort is spent trying to understand the purpose of the operation or why the operation exists at all.

Given the task of reducing the costs of the paperwork in an office, most managers will try to develop more efficient ways of processing the volume of reports. The cost effective manager, on the other hand, will first ask *why* each of the reports is needed. He may find that a significant portion of the volume is no longer required. By simply eliminating the unnecessary, he will accomplish the cost reduction task.

Many believe that information is self-organizing; i.e., that one has only to continue collecting data and eventually it must sort itself into the necessary information from which they can make the right decision. Even if this were true it is still an extremely wasteful and expensive process compared with the approach of first determining what information is needed and then expending effort to develop only that small amount of detail.

Before we discuss the Six-Step Cost Management Approach it is important that we understand the term Cost Management and its elements—Avoidance, Prevention, Elimination and Reduction.

Cost Avoidance

When we avoid costs we put off spending which normally would have occurred. It is a deliberate decision *not* to take some action which would have caused some costs to be incurred.

Cost avoidance can be profitable if applied to the right area, but can also result in increased costs if misapplied.

When you go to the grocery store and *avoid* buying luxury foods, i.e., candy, specially packaged items, those items generally referred to as impulse purchases, you are ahead of the game. Also in the office, *avoiding* the temptation to staff for the peak workload, and relying on temporary help or limited overtime can keep costs down.

But avoiding needed repairs to equipment in either the home or business which result in more costly repairs later is false economy.

To evaluate whether a particular cost can be avoided, you have to decide whether there is a real need to make the expenditure, or is it something that would just be nice to do. If there is a definite need, then the actual expenditure should be kept to a minimum using other cost management techniques, but it is not a candidate for cost avoidance.

The following are examples of cost avoidance:

1. Scheduling vacations during slow periods to avoid the need for temporary help or overtime.
2. Discontinuing the practice of buying office supplies for certain departments or individuals because of their personal preference which is different from the office standard.

3. Avoiding telephone calls when a telegram or letter would suffice.
4. Limiting telephone conversation. Most telephone calls over three minutes are ripe candidates.
5. Avoiding overtime by better planning or placing orders earlier.
6. Not making extra copies of reports, just in case they might be needed.
7. Avoiding changes of company name or logo formats.
8. Using a typing pool instead of private secretaries.
9. Not using First Class travel when Tourist class is available.
10. Handwritten notes rather than formal memos.
11. Avoiding First Class postage on bulk mailings.
12. Limiting the number of employees attending trade shows.
13. Avoiding too high an approval required on routine transactions.
14. Batching telex messages on paper tape for transmission on a single minimum connection time.

As you can see from the examples, cost avoidance candidates are costs which are incurred to satisfy a personal desire of someone in the business or because of an employee's lack of understanding that the cost could be avoided. The items listed are only examples. In every business today there are hundreds of such unnecessary costs being incurred. Many of them are the result of individual employee actions of which the manager has only vague awareness.

Cost Prevention

Cost prevention is a process of thoroughly evaluating individual actions and total programs in advance so that you don't spend the money unless the result is *sure* to be profitable, or *sure* to achieve other indirect objectives which contribute to the overall profitability of the company.

To be most effective, a cost prevention program must be a *continuing* evaluation of new projects, staff additions, organizational expansions, and similar actions which create costs in order to make each cost prove its anticipated contribution to the profitability of the operation.

It may be obvious to everyone that a $50,000 advertising campaign designed to generate additional sales margins of $40,000 is not a worthwhile program. However, most projects are not so obvious; for example, take a reorganization which adds three new highly paid managers. Only a close examination will determine if the expected results can justify the additional overhead.

Cost Elimination

Cost elimination is an "after-the-fact" action. A cost elimination program looks at the operations as they are today and asks the question, "What can we get rid of to improve profitability?"

To eliminate means to do away with permanently. This principle can be applied to a whole plant which is unprofitable, a single product, or simply a past procedure that has outlived its usefulness.

For example, take the product which is losing money. The sales department will quickly point out that it is needed to complete the line, to satisfy certain customers, or several other very good reasons why it should be continued.

But when you look at the cold hard facts, the product is a loser. Only three possible alternatives are available: Raise the price to a level which will provide a proper margin; reduce the cost of producing it; or eliminate it from your product line.

Reducing the production cost won't work if you have been practicing normal cost management techniques. Raising the price may give more of the volume to your competition so that they can lose money on it; but that still leaves certain of its fixed costs to be absorbed by a lower volume. The only sound action is to get rid of it completely and concentrate your efforts on those products which are paying your salary.

Many functions and procedures which were established

in the past for very good reasons often outlive their usefulness.

Cost elimination techniques get rid of these "sleeper" operations and "sacred cows." Don't feel bad when you find them; every organization has a few. Remember, your operations are developed and run by employees who are human, like you and me.

Cost Reduction

Cost reduction programs are the most talked about and least effective method of the cost management techniques. There has been such a proliferation of books on cost reduction in recent years that this topic has purposely been selected for the last sub-title.

When we talk about cost reduction it usually means we have already let our operations get fat. As a result, cost reduction is hastily put in motion on a crash basis with temporary results. The most effective cost reduction techniques are those which are carefully and deliberately worked out. Value analysis, staff reviews, and work simplification programs are practiced by some companies. However, many times these programs are not conducted in conjunction with the day-to-day management functions. Since the line manager may be only partially involved and seldom has any personal commitment, he may take other independent actions that more than offset the results of such programs. It is amazing how much energy is spent developing cost reductions for functions or products which should have been eliminated in the first place. It is usually more effective when you start a cost reduction program to apply cost elimination techniques first and save yourself a lot of wasted effort.

However, if you have allowed costs to get out of control and there just isn't time to effect a comprehensive cost management program, then short term cost reduction goals may be appropriate until you resume control and are able to start applying overall cost management techniques. Be sure that the cost reduction program establishes measureable goals as well as a schedule for monitoring progress during the length of the program. The absolutely worst goal you can select is an across the board percentage cut in costs. It is unfair, impractical, and in the long run ineffective. You will probably get some reduction in costs but most managers usually find ways to be granted exemptions of one sort or another.

Cost Management

Cost management uses all the techniques and methods of cost avoidance, cost prevention, cost elimination, and cost reduction. It is a total program, not aimed at the short-term problem of reducing costs; but rather aimed at the long-term objective of minimizing and controlling costs throughout the organization.

A cost management program is unlike normal budgeting and profit planning used by many companies, in that it requires managers to find improved ways of running their operations, not just following past methods. Such plans not only aim at overall company objectives, but also specific cost improvement goals.

Cost management requires managers to be cost conscious every day, not just when they receive orders to implement a cost reduction program. Cost management is an attitude which must be developed every day until it becomes a habit as strong as getting up in the morning to go to work. The company that trains its managers to be cost conscious and to manage their costs has a leg up on all its competitors.

Cost management requires three general goals, in addition to the objectives normally assigned to managers:

1. To make the present operations more effective.
2. To find the real potential in the operations.
3. To insure an increase in profitability which assures a future for the company and the manager.

An effective Cost Management Approach requires concentration on those few areas where improvement in performance will have a significant impact on the profitability of the operation. That is, on those activities where a relatively minor increase in efficiency will produce a major increase in economic effectiveness.

Cost Management is not a technique which can be learned at once and usefully applied thereafter. Cost Management is an attitude and a habit of mind. The various techniques described are intended to bring about an awareness of cost management methods. There is no sudden conversion from a belief that costs are necessary to a belief that many costs can be eliminated. Cost Management is a matter of awareness and practice by the manager, then sharing that awareness and practice with his subordinates and peers.

The following is a simple six-step approach to help managers develop their own cost management skills.

The Six Simple Steps

Step One
—Acquire a Cost Management Attitude.

Step Two
—Analyze and Understand Your Operations

Step Three
—Evaluate Your Operations by Asking the Right Questions.

Step Four
—Turn the Problems in Your Operations into Opportunities by Developing Cost Improvement Ideas.

Step Five
—Turn Your Cost Improvement Ideas into Profits by Taking Action to Avoid, Prevent and Eliminate Unnecessary Costs.

Step Six
—Expand Your Cost Improvement ideas into a continuing Cost Management Program with the help of your subordinates and the other managers in your company.

This six-step approach is not a magic formula which will enable you to solve all the cost problems you will face as a Manager in a business. It is a springboard, a beginning for your development and advancement as a manager of costs and the operations that cause them.

It is an enormous loss to the world and to the individual that so many managers spend several years of their careers, sometimes their entire career, before they develop basic techniques to manage the costs for which they are responsible.

I must emphasize the all important point that the six-step cost management approach is a method, a format to help you find, develop and exploit the cost improvement opportunities in your operations. Cost problems are not solved by books such as this. They are solved in some manager's head. Methods and techniques simply get that manager's head turned in the right direction so that he can focus on the solution.

Use this method to aid you in the development of your cost management skills. As those skills grow you will find by experience how to modify it to suit your individual management style and environment.

Some managers require a detailed understanding of a given operation in order to develop a better, less costly approach; others need only limited information to create the ideas for major cost improvements.

Some operations cry out for immediate changes to improve cost effectiveness, while others require in-depth study before decisions can be made.

Expand, contract, and modify this six-step approach to suit the circumstances which surround you and your operations.

Developing Your Cost Management Abilities

A person isn't born with a fixed ability for cost management. Rather, he has as much skill as he has had interest and opportunity to develop. Few people have a natural aptitude for cost management, but everyone can develop this ability if they deliberately seek it. Most business schools have no specific programs to encourage cost management habits, although they may teach many of the mechanical techniques of cost control. Later application of these mechanical techniques in the practical business world disillusions even the best from each graduating class because they haven't developed the attitude and habits that make them work.

Real life operations are not measured by examination questions on textbook theory, but rather measurement is by the dollar and cents results of profit or loss.

To develop your cost management skills start by evaluating your attitude toward costs, as outlined in Chapter 2. Then, expand your approach into a cost improvement attitude.

Opening Your Mind to Cost Improvement Ideas

The first step is to keep your mind open. Look around you and start noting the cost improvement opportunities. Loosen up your thinking so that opportunities to cut costs won't be blocked by preconceived ideas or conclusions. Make it a habit to keep your thoughts objective and your senses alert and receptive; for you never quite know where or when a cost improvement idea will come to you. The fact that you are reading this book is an indication you are searching.

Cultivating a Cost Improvement Atmosphere

People around you can have a tremendous influence on your thinking and attitude. That is why you often find creative individuals preferring to be in the company of similarly talented individuals. In most companies, however, you are not usually in control of who will be your immediate associates, unless you are in a position to replace those who don't have a cost conscious attitude. Even if you could fill your office with creative individuals, they may not possess the technical skills needed. Therefore, you must convince those around you to develop cost conscious attitudes. Encourage them to think about costs and to discuss their cost improvement ideas. Help them to implement those ideas that have merit.

A cost conscious attitude can be contagious. When one person is recognized for developing and implementing cost improvements, others take note and also start to make suggestions. Once they have experienced the thrill of seeing their ideas recognized and used, they tend to talk about it with others. Soon a chain reaction begins to occur and everyone wants to get involved. Those who don't soon find they are in the minority and either leave or stay out of the way.

It is difficult at first to develop such a cost conscious atmosphere, but if you are determined and set an example it can spread like "wild fire."

Start small by developing the people who work directly for you and then expand by working with others from other departments. Remember, when you start to expand, you already have your people as ambassadors to help influence others in the company.

You have heard the expression, "A picture is worth a thousand words." Developing and implementing a good cost improvement idea is a concrete example of what is possible and can be more effective than words or pictures. So start in your own department and encourage others and eventually your attitude and accomplishments will have their effect in other areas throughout the company.

Review of Step One

Let's summarize and review the first step in the six-step Cost Management Approach—Acquiring a Cost Management Attitude:

1. Expand and develop your cost conscious attitude.
2. Understand the elements of Cost Management— Avoidance, Prevention, Elimination and Reduction.
3. Keep your mind open to new ideas and concepts, and avoid mental blocks put there by preconceived conclusions.

4. Cultivate a cost improvement atmosphere.

The development of a Cost Management Attitude is more important in reaping the long-range benefits from a Cost Management Program than any of the other five steps. Without the proper attitude which is receptive to the concepts and techniques outlined in the following pages, fully effective Cost Management is difficult, if not impossible. Absorb this first step and you will be more than halfway toward becoming an effective cost conscious manager.

4 ANALYZING AND UNDERSTANDING YOUR OPERATIONS

Almost any problem presents a cost improvement opportunity. For example, as a sales manager how can you increase sales in your company? You might take the obvious approach of adding more salesmen and with them their related costs; or, you could develop ideas to increase the effectiveness of your present salesmen and distributors, thus getting the increased volume without increasing costs.

As an employee who wants a raise, you might simply ask for an increase and get a little more money or none at all. Or, you could develop some cost improvement ideas that show the company how to make more profit. Employees who are constantly developing cost improvement ideas are very valuable to a company. As their value increases, the company is usually happy to reward them with salary increases as well as other forms of recognition. To get a job or to get an advance, first show your value by recognizing cost improvement opportunities and implementing creative ideas to exploit them.

Even at home there are many cost improvement opportunities all around you waiting to be explored to increase the financial status and enjoyment of your family. Consider something as simple as turning off unnecessary electrical lights and appliances, keeping the temperature a degree or two lower in the winter and higher in the summer, or making less frequent trips to the store in the family car. All of these conserve energy and reduce utility costs. Saving energy around the house can have a significant impact on a family's resources in these days of ever increasing utility costs.

Every business has literally thousands of potential cost improvement opportunities. Many could make a significant impact on the profits of the operation.

Why then do these opportunities go unnoticed? For the most part managers don't take advantage of cost improvement opportunities which surround them because they are unaware of them.

As a manager interested in finding ways to improve profits, your first step should be to understand and analyze the operations which you are currently responsible for. What better place to start than in your own department? It is there that you are in a position to implement cost improvement ideas with a minimum of interference from other people. What better place to "try your wings."

Understanding Your Operations

Do you understand completely the department or operating unit you manage? Why does the department exist at all? What functions is it expected to perform and why are they necessary? What functions is it *not* expected to perform? How do the functions of the department interrelate with other departments in the organization? How do they contribute to the overall objectives of the company? How is the department organized? What are the capabilities of the individuals who perform the departmental duties and activities? What are the detail policies and procedures being followed? What detail methods are being used to execute those policies and procedures? Do you have specific strategies, plans, and programs to discharge your responsibilities?

These questions may sound academic but it is surprising how many managers really don't know what is happening in their area of responsibility. "That may be true of a newly appointed manager," you say, "but the manager who has been on the job for awhile knows everything that is happening and why."

If you believe that, ask yourself these questions. "When was the last time I took the time to review the organization, purpose and strategy of the department I am responsible for? Are the policies and procedures *being followed* the same as the policies and procedures *I think* are being followed?"

Let's be honest. Most managers are too busy with day-to-day problems, telephone calls, staff meetings, special reports and other time-consuming activities to get involved with such details. After all, isn't everyone busy! They must be doing something useful. *You* are, however, the person responsible for managing those people. Shouldn't *you* know in detail what everyone is doing and why?

Every activity, every action taken by the people who work for you generates costs. Costs must be paid for with either increased sales prices or reduced profits. To manage those costs you must understand all the activities you are responsible for in sufficient detail to avoid, prevent, and eliminate costs which do not contribute to your department's or your company's objectives.

But how, with the busy schedule every manager seems to have, can a manager get into that amount of detail?

It will take some of the manager's time. No doubt about it. But then isn't that what the manager should be doing in the first place?

Start by setting aside a period of time. Hold the telephone calls, avoid meetings if possible and push aside all those other special projects. Take the time to make a complete Cost Management Review of your department. It could be the most important and best spent time in your career.

The Cost Management Review

A cost management review can be broken into several sub-reviews. Among them are the organization review, the system review, the function review, the staff review, and the program review. Although these terms are to some degree self-explanatory, a brief explanation of each type may be helpful.

The Organization Review

The Organization Review examines the structure and purpose of the department or company. Its purpose is to determine the unit's objectives together with its basic strategy and programs to achieve those objectives. It starts with an evaluation of how the department's objectives contribute to the overall effectiveness of the company. It then develops new objectives to replace those found to be taking the department away from its appointed purpose. This type review also examines current reporting procedures, intra-department chains of command, and the structure of the various work sections to determine whether or not they are making a maximum contribution to the achievement of the department and company goals. In general, it is a review of what each department is doing, why it is doing it, and how it is organized to do it. When the results of the review are compared to what higher management *thought* the department was doing, the manager knows the effectiveness of his operation.

For instance, an organizational review of the sales department might point out that their organization and its objectives are aimed at increasing only sales volume, whereas the company's prime objective may be to introduce a new line of more profitable products. The new line is expected to result in lower sales volumes initially with higher margins. This is directly opposite of the objectives of the sales department, which is to concentrate its salesmen's efforts toward reducing mark-ups on the old line of products in order to gain a greater share of a competitive market.

The organization review looks at the big picture to determine if the department's efforts are focused on the right objective. Is the department traveling in the same direction as the rest of the company, or have they taken a detour which conflicts with the overall company objectives?

Remember, a department can be as small as one person. Let's take a hypothetical example to show how even one individual can work hard at the wrong objective and not realize it.

The XYZ Company

Joe Smith is a salesman with the XYZ Company. In fact, he is its only salesman in their Atlanta Branch. The president has given him the management objective of increasing the sales this year by 20%. "They must be profitable sales, however," cautions his boss.

Joe works hard; he travels more; he entertains more lavishly to improve relations with the more difficult customers. He pursues the smaller accounts and extends more liberal credit terms in order to penetrate deeper into the available market. Joe gets the 20% increase in sales and after three months the president calls him in for a little talk.

"Joe, your sales are up and it looks like you will have no trouble meeting the sales objective. However, I am concerned about the profitability of these increased sales."

A look of surprise comes to Joe's face. "What do you mean? The gross margin is only slightly less than last year, but isn't that to be expected when you're trying to buck the competition?"

"It's not the gross margin that's the problem. In fact, you have done a good job of maintaining our usual margins on the products. But the additional sales are not really profitable to the company," replies the president.

"I don't understand how you can say that," retorts Joe. "Your evaluation is contradictory. If the sales are up and margins are approximately the same, that has to increase profits. I've really worked my tail off the last three months."

The president opens a report on his desk.

"Well, let's look at the overall picture," the president replies. "Last year you sold about $500,000 of products with a 20% margin, giving us about $100,000 at the gross margin level. Your salary and travel expenses totaled about $50,000 leaving the company $50,000 to cover the other operating expenses such as shipping and billing, interest to finance the receivable balances and other administrative costs. Our administration costs last year were approximately 5% of sales, or $25,000 on your sales level last year. That left a $25,000 profit before income taxes, or about 5% on sales. Based on our capital invested, that was about a 10% return before income taxes on the stockholders' investment."

"Based on your first three months sales results, it looks like you will bring in about $600,000 in sales this year. Just about on your goal of a 20% increase. However, your travel expenses are running well over last year; and, if we project the first three months, it looks like your salary and expenses will be close to $60,000 this year. With a 20% margin that means that your $600,000 of sales will generate $120,000 gross margin, less your expenses will leave $60,000 for other overhead expenses. That still looks good if our administrative costs had remained at 5% or $30,000. But they haven't. Because of the size of the orders you have been accepting, the volume of billings has increased substantially, which meant putting on an additional billing clerk whose salary, together with her various fringe benefits, cost us $10,000. Those extra credit terms you have been extending to your new customers, have also caused our investment in receivables to increase and the smaller orders have increased our shipping costs."

"In summary, if we consider all the costs of your increased sales, they have not only eliminated the 20% margin generated, but they have also offset the net profit you used to make on your lower sales volume."

"I just can't believe that," countered Joe. "Can you recap it for me?"

"Let me compare it for you," said the president, drawing a pad of paper across the desk.

THE XYZ COMPANY—ATLANTA BRANCH
COMPARISON OF NET PROFIT BETWEEN YEARS

	Actual Last Year		Projected This Year	
	Amount	*%*	*Amount*	*%*
Sales	$500,000	100%	$600,000	100%
Cost of Products	400,000	80%	480,000	80%
Gross Margin	100,000	20%	120,000	20%
Direct Selling Cost (Joe's Expenses)	50,000	10%	60,000	10%
Administrative Costs	25,000	5%	30,000	5%
Extra Clerk to Handle Volume			10,000	
Extra Shipping Costs			5,000	
Total Expenses	75,000		105,000	
Net Profit Before Taxes	25,000		15,000	
Average Investment	$250,000		$275,000	
Return on Investment	10%		5.5%	

"As you can see, Joe," said the president, "The stockholders could put their money in a 6% savings account and make a better return with less risk."

Joe really didn't understand his objectives. He also didn't understand that cost management means *all* costs, not just the ones which affect gross margin.

Understanding your operations means understanding the effects that the actions taken by you can have on other costs in the company. In Joe's case, he didn't understand that changing the company's basic sales policies by accepting smaller orders and extending extra credit terms, had dramatically increased administrative costs as well as the cost of invested capital. His objectives were focused on sales and gross margins only, a narrow view that many salesmen seem to have.

Formal vs. Implied Objectives

Most departments establish *formal* objectives which are agreed upon by the Manager and his superior. In the example, Joe's formal objectives were as follows:

1. Improve the company's image with customers.
2. Increase sales by 20%.
3. Maintain margins on sales at 20%.
4. Keep sales expenses at approximately 10% of sales or less.

The problem is that the objectives of a given department or function are much more numerous than those which we tend to list formally. Each department has another vast set of objectives which are implied and therefore usually not discussed. Some of Joe's implied objectives were as follows:

1. Sell to customers who will pay their bills.
2. Promote larger quantity orders to keep shipment and clerical costs down.
3. Promote the quality of XYZ products.
4. Develop marketing survey information for forecasting.

This list of implied objectives could go on and on. The point is that there are a whole host of very important day-to-day objectives which every manager must meet just to keep the business running smoothly.

It is in this vast list of implied objectives that you will find the greatest opportunities of improvement. Generally, these objectives are not in writing, even in large sophisticated companies. It is assumed that they are obvious and therefore putting them in writing is a waste of time. These objectives are usually passed on from manager to manager and employee to employee by word of mouth. It is these day-to-day objectives that many managers forget about when they are evaluating their operations, and it is these objectives which will cause major problems in the operations of a company if not achieved. When was the last time you heard top management praise lower supervision for meeting these implied objectives? Yet, when these implied objectives are not met, major dents can occur in the profitability of an operation.

Keep in mind the implied objectives when you make your organization review. They are more important in most cases than the formal objectives which everyone talks about and puts in the "five year plan."

Start your analysis of your operations with an organizational review to be sure you understand your objectives and how those objectives interrelate with the other operations in the company. Next, make a Systems Review of your department.

The Systems Review

The Systems Review looks at the policies and procedures in operation in a department or company. Examples would be, a review of the internal control procedures of the Treasury Department, or the methods used by the Personnel Department to recruit and train new employees.

First, understand what is being done and why. If the company has a policy of selling only to distributors rather than directly to the ultimate customer, find out why. Perhaps experience has shown that local servicing of the product can be done effectively only by local representation, rather than a factory representative. Failure to understand this might cause you to accept an order on a direct customer basis only to find out later that it is impossible for the company to service the customer. The resulting costs would far exceed any margins on the original sale.

Some companies have policy and procedure manuals. If there is one for your department, study it. Ask questions on anything you don't understand. Be sure you understand both the objectives of the policy and how it is monitored to assure compliance. Don't concern yourself with whether you agree or disagree with the policy; that comes later when you fully understand all the reasons why there is such a policy. If you have some doubts about it, jot them down for later reference when you get to the evaluation stage of your program.

If the company doesn't have written policies and procedures you will have to work even harder. If you are a new manager, take notes of discussions you have with the various individuals who are teaching you and pay close attention to be sure you understand completely. It will take you longer to understand the policies and procedures if they aren't written, so perhaps one of your first cost improvement ideas will be to get them in written form for your department. This will save valuable time in the future and assure continuity when new employees enter your operations.

If you have been managing your department for sometime, outline your operating policies and procedures and then discuss them in detail with your boss. Be sure that both of you agree with the mode of operation before you proceed to finalize your operating strategy.

When reviewing the various procedures you may find it helpful to flow chart (or have one of your subordinates flow chart) the various paperwork so there will be no mistake as to exactly how the procedure works.

As you study each policy and procedure make sure that is what is really happening. Many times policy and procedure manuals become outdated. What the manual may state is happening, may not be what is actually taking place. Remember the objective of a systems review is to determine and understand what is *actually happening* today.

If you find things taking place which are not covered by the current policies and procedures, make a note of them for later evaluation. Unless there is a critical breach of policy, don't try to make a change now. Your objective is to learn and to understand. You will be in a better position to evaluate and recommend changes after you understand the whole picture.

You may find that your operations cover several functions. To fully review and understand them is going to be a major task. Don't give up. It is not as difficult as it may seem. Divide the department into its various functions and study one at a time, thus using the old principle of "Divide and Conquer."

Next make a function review of your operations.

The Function Review

The Function Review examines the extent to which a department or the individuals within it are actually performing the work which has been assigned. For instance, a function review of the marketing department would insure that this group is performing all the duties expected of it, but is not pursuing those assigned to the Engineering and Manufacturing Departments such as product design or manufacturing methods. In some organizations, for example, marketing has so much influence over product design and manufacture that though the company has very happy customers, they are unable to make a profit on the resulting products.

Ask yourself, "Is my department performing all the functions and duties that would normally be expected of this type department? Are we performing duties which would normally be performed by some other department? If we are not performing all the expected duties, who is?

If we are performing duties outside our normal function, are we duplicating someone else's effort?"

In small companies you are apt to find considerable overlap of functions, since the number of managers is limited. Make sure you are not trying to do someone else's job. Also, advise others if they are expending efforts on duties that your people are responsible for.

In larger companies functions become highly structured, even so, a function review often reveals many duplications of effort.

Remember, you are trying to understand just what is happening. Make notes as you discover possible opportunities for improvement, but wait until you have the whole picture before you start the evaluation process.

At this point you should have a pretty good understanding of your department's objectives, the policies and procedures being followed, and the functions you are responsible for. The next step is a detail Staffing Review.

The Staffing Review

The Staffing Review is a detail study of *what* each individual in a department is doing, together with an evaluation of each activity to determine how it contributes to the overall benefit of the department or company. Such reviews also develop measurements of output for repetitive operations in order to balance workloads, eliminate bottlenecks, and sometimes eliminate excess staff.

The real benefit from a staffing review is that it generally identifies a number of obsolete procedures, methods, and operations that can be eliminated. The wasted efforts can then be redirected to other activities with greater opportunities.

"People costs" many times represent one-third or more of the total overhead costs of an operation. A concentrated study of staffing requirements is an essential part of any well planned Cost Management Review. Ask yourself, "How many jobs are there in my operation which started with the business and no longer are necessary to achieve my current objectives?"

Some management consulting firms, in order to sell top management on employing them at substantial fees, will quickly quote potential dollar savings equal to ten to twenty percent of salary costs. But why pay a management consultant 50% to 100% of the first year's savings to perform on a crash basis that which should be done daily by the company's own management? Make your own staffing review and avoid unnecessary consultant fees.

Because of the detail nature of a staffing review, it is best to have a definite program and procedure to follow. This makes it possible for your people to do most of the detail fact gathering, thus leaving your time free for analysis and evaluation.

Staffing Review Example

The objective of a staffing review is to increase operating profitability by studying current departmental activities in detail in order to:

1. Improve operating methods and procedures.
2. Eliminate non-essential work activities.
3. Identify and implement needed additional services.
4. Utilize employee abilities and potential to the fullest.
5. Complement existing programs and policies.

The basic approach of this review is to define existing work activities, to study those activities for better understanding, to evaluate them, to develop improved methods and procedures, and then to take the necessary steps should changes be indicated.

The defining stage of the review is accomplished by using an activity list worksheet form on which each individual employee, with the help of his supervisor, describes his work activities. He should classify them according to type and importance, indicate the frequency that the activity is required, estimate times needed to accomplish the tasks, and then project the expected volume during a given period.

After the activity lists are completed and summarized,

the manager and his supervisors are in a position to study each activity within their department to determine:

1. The objective of the activity.
2. Its importance in relation to all the activities of the department.
3. The total volume of work the activity represents.
4. The time requirements of the activity.
5. How frequent the activity occurs.
6. The complexity of the individual tasks.
7. Who has been assigned the activity.

After they have completed their study of the activity lists, the manager and his supervisors should be able to evaluate the existing work activities to:

1. Discover activities that do not contribute to the department objectives.
2. Discover activities that should be performed that are not being performed.
3. Identify cost improvement opportunities for activities which can be made more effective.

The last step in the review is to take any action necessary to implement programs that capitalize on the cost improvement opportunities identified.

Unless the department is a very small one, most managers find it advantageous to assign an individual to coordinate the review and assist the manager in summarizing and evaluating the data. This same individual can also train the employees and supervisors and assist them as needed in completing the activities list worksheets.

The following pages show a sample Activity List and set of Employee Instructions.

The XYZ Company
Operations Improvement Program
Employee Activity List Instructions

Attached is an activity form we are requesting each employee to complete. The purpose of the activity list form is to provide management with information on the extent of our efforts in each function. Our objective is to review thoroughly our operations. After evaluation, workloads may be shifted in order to place the heaviest emphasis on the most important functions we perform. We anticipate that this review will also enable your supervisor not only to develop a better balance in workloads between individuals, but also to develop improved methods and procedures which should make your job more interesting.

The way in which the activities are listed will depend on the type of department being analyzed. Since the form was developed for use throughout the company, the instructions have been written to cover the larger departments being analyzed where summarization will be done by computer. Smaller departments may delete certain steps or improvise shortcuts in order to reduce the time required to accumulate the information.

Check with your supervisor about any possible changes to be made for your department. Please read these instructions carefully before proceeding. If you have any questions, please ask your supervisor for assistance.

Instructions

The following guidelines and instructions are designed to assist employees and supervisors in filling out the employee activity list. An activity list form is attached for procedure reference.

1. General Guidelines

Printing
All information entered on the activity list should be printed.

OPERATIONS IMPROVEMENT PROGRAM

ACTIVITY LIST

NAME: _____
TITLE: _____
EMPLOYEE NO. _____
CONTROL NO. _____

COST CENTER _____
DATE _____

ACT. NO.	PRIOR	CAT.	ACTIVITY DESCRIPTION	UNIT OF MEASURE	FREQ.	ESTIMATE TIME MINUTES	VOLUME	REQ'D. WEEKLY

Entries in Pencil

Entries in pencil are encouraged to facilitate any necessary changes.

Neat and Legible

As the information on an activity sheet will be reviewed by the supervisor and coordinator, and later keypunched, it is important that entries be neat and legible.

Correct Number of Spaces

In the instructions that follow, please note the maximum number of field positions assigned to each respective form column or descriptive space. Use of only the correct number of spaces is necessary to aid mechanical summarization of the information.

Employee Definition

In the instructions that follow the term *employee* will refer to the person listing his or her activities.

II. *Activity List Heading*

Name

Name is entered by the employee. There is no restriction on the number of spaces required as this information will not be keypunched.

Title

Job Title is entered by the employee. There is no restriction on the number of spaces required as this information will not be keypunched.

Employee Number

Employee will enter his regularly assigned *employee number*.

Control Number

The *control number* is entered by the supervisor. This is a three digit code number to identify the department manager and supervisor of the employee preparing the activity list.

Cost Center

Employee enters his regularly assigned *cost center* number.

Date

The space provided for the *date* is to be left blank. A date will be entered at the time the activity sheet is batched for keypunching.

III. *Activity Description and Related Data*

Activity Number

The *activity number* is entered by the employee. This number is for activity reference only. There is no significance to the order in which activities are listed. Maximum number of field positions—two (2).

Priority

The space provided for *priority* is to be left blank. It will be used later when the activities are evaluated by the supervisor.

Category

The *category number* is entered by the supervisor. This is a number to classify an activity for later summary reporting. Category descriptions and numbers will be developed for each department prior to program implementation and have been distributed with these instructions. If you did not receive the listing for your department, please ask your supervisor for a copy. Maximum number of field positions—two (2).

Activity Description

The *activity description* is entered by the employee taking into consideration the following definitions and description guidelines:

Definitions:

An *activity* is a readily definable task made up of a series of work elements.

An *element* is a unit of work with easily identified start and stop points.

Guidelines:

Usually the first word in an activity description is an action verb.

Example: (1) *Audit* an expense report, (2) *Pre-*pare absentee report, (3) *Type* letter, (4) *Process* shop orders, etc.

Description Fieldlength—The maximum number of field positions for the activity description is thirty-six (36). Therefore, description should be concise and if necessary, abbreviated.

Unit of Measure

The unit of measure is entered by the employee. It is the common denominator for measurements and assignment of work activities. In some instances, a trial and error approach is necessary to determine the most practical unit of measure. For example: Numbers of invoices processed, numbers of purchase orders prepared, or numbers of letters typed. Maximum number of field positions—ten (10).

Frequency

The *frequency* or rate of activity occurrence is entered by the employee. The following coding is to be used to indicate activity frequency:

D - Daily
B - Biweekly
W - Weekly
M - Monthly
Q - Quarterly
S - Semiannually
A - Annually
X - Special

Estimate Time Minutes

The *estimated time* to complete one unit of activity is entered on the activity list by the supervisor. The time estimate itself will be developed by the employee

Important! There is a maximum of five (5) field positions provided for estimated time—four (4) digits plus the decimal point. Each estimated time entry should be expressed to the nearest tenth of a minute. Even estimates that are whole numbers such as 15 minutes should be entered 15.0.

Volume

Activity *volume* is entered by the supervisor, however, volume figures will be developed jointly between the employees and supervisor. When practical, it is best to estimate volume by actual count. Maximum number of field positions—five (5).

Important! It is imperative that the volume entry correspond with the stated frequency. For example, if the activity frequency is daily; the volume must be expressed as *daily volume*.

Required Weekly

The equivalent weekly time requirement (Required weekly) is automatically extended by computer program as follows: Frequency X conversion factor X estimated time X volume = *Weekly Time Requirement*.

Note: The *Conversion Factor* is the number that converts activity time (based on original frequency) to a weekly basis. For example, an activity performed monthly would be divided by four (4); a daily activity would be multiplied by five (5) to establish weekly time requirement.

For those who want to manually convert frequencies to a weekly basis, the following schedule will apply:

FREQUENCY CONVERSION

Week	5 days
Biweekly	10 days
Month	4 weeks
Quarter	13 weeks
Semi-annual	26 weeks
Annual	52 weeks

The staffing review not only gives the manager a wealth of information for developing cost improvement ideas, but also gives him volume information for determining the true amount of staffing required to perform the current activities of his department. With this volume information he can determine what the work load will be at various levels of business activity. By comparing current volumes to current staffing levels he may find immediate savings available by transferring excess staff to other jobs in the company. This same volume information is also helpful in evaluating potential savings of effort if certain activities were eliminated. It is not unusual for a thorough staffing review to reveal savings of ten percent or more.

The Program Review

The Program Review, sometimes called "Zero Base Budgeting," appraises the value of specific departments or company programs which are planned or have been implemented.

This type of review is best made before a new program is undertaken, thus preventing costs rather than trying to reduce them. However, it can be used to review existing programs to determine if the originally anticipated benefits have actually happened. For example, comparing the actual savings to projected savings resulting from a capital improvement; or another example, evaluating the results from a new advertising approach.

Project type costs are expenditures which directly relate to doing or not doing some specific endeavor. Whether the specific project is completed or not will not generally interfere with the other operations of the business. Project type costs must be evaluated on the basis of what benefit the specific project will contribute to the objectives of the business. If the benefits which accrue are not sufficient to justify the cost of the project, then the project should be discontinued.

Basically, the program review calls for the comparison of all costs associated with that project to the tangible and intangible benefits being generated by the project. All the projects for a given department or company are then compared with each other and ranked according to importance and pay-off value. The manager can then quantitatively decide which projects should be dropped depending upon how great his need is to avoid or eliminate costs.

Summary

The above types of reviews are examples of studies which, taken as a whole, can bring to the manager the type of information he needs to understand and analyze his operations. They provide information he will not get from the usual flow of management data being prepared in companies today. They also provide a basis for him to evaluate his current operations so that he can develop improvement ideas to make his function more cost effective.

Each of these reviews is aimed to find out exactly what *is* happening, not what the manager *thinks* is happening. The manager who is able to conduct an effective and objective Cost Management Review of his operations will find that he has at his disposal the information necessary to streamline operations and eliminate unnecessary costs.

As you review and analyze, ask these questions; "Do I know what I am spending on various items? Where are the major expenses generated? Why do I need to spend the money? and, Who is causing each expense to be incurred?"

Many of us don't take the time to think about our operations in those terms. We only think we do but we really are too busy trying to make more money than taking a close look at where the money goes. The Cost Management Review which is made up of its many sub-reviews will give you the necessary understanding of your operations to answer the above questions. It will also point out many problems with your operations you didn't realize existed.

But remember, problems can be cost improvement opportunities.

If you recognize and tackle every problem as a possible cost improvement opportunity, you will soon be winning praise for yourself and dollars for your pocket. You will develop an attitude of thinking which will enable you to recognize even greater opportunities. Once you can say with complete assurance, "I understand my operations," you have made important headway and you will be in a position to exploit the opportunities. You will be recognized as someone who has the ability to manage costs so that every dollar counts.

An effective Cost Management Review Program must be a long-range commitment, not a crash effort to deal with an unexpected emergency. Costs, reasons for incurring them, their relationship to the benefits they produce, and the necessity of incurring them, must be continually reviewed for the purpose of recognizing the changing relationship of each department's functions and activities.

Changing business conditions require constant vigilance. The Cost Management Review Program used last year with good results may not identify this year's problems. Managers must continually search for new techniques and methods to avoid, eliminate and reduce costs. For this reason, a Cost Management Review Program must be flexible and adaptable to new circumstances as they arise.

A Cost Management Review Program is exactly what its name implies. It is a program and not a panacea. It will probably not be 100% effective. Continued management attention however, and follow-up on information provided by even a modest program can result in substantial profit improvements.

The purpose of understanding the facts is to be able to make them work for you. In the next chapter we will discuss ways to evaluate your operations.

5 EVALUATING YOUR OPERATIONS

Before discussing step three in the Six-Step Cost Management approach, it is important that we fully understand what is meant by the terms "cost" and "cost improvement."

What Are Costs?

Costs can be directly visible; that is, those that you pay and record as you go along; i.e., purchases of material, wages and salaries, and other expenses which are paid each month. These are what most managers think of when discussing costs.

Costs are also sometimes indirectly visible, but nonetheless very real. Breakage, theft and spoilage are inventory costs which eventually show up as inventory adjustments of one kind or another. Bad debts on receivables, fixed assets which are not utilized yet tie-up capital and loss of employee time and effort because of low morale or ineffective working conditions are examples of these indirectly visible costs. The "White Collar Thief" is often able to cover the true cost of having him on the payroll; many are never discovered.

As you evaluate your operations, keep in mind that improvements which help to prevent or eliminate indirectly visible costs are just as important, sometimes more important, than improvements which attack directly visible costs.

71

Improvements in procedures which result in better control and utilization of the company's cash, receivables, inventories, and other assets can be very effective in contributing to profitability. Don't miss this area of opportunity when you are evaluating your operations.

What Is a Cost Improvement?

Cost improvement in an operation results from two basic actions; eliminating activities and costs which do not contribute to the profitability of the company, thus reducing actual cost; or, making the operation more effective so that productivity is increased without increasing costs. For example; you could eliminate excessive telephone equipment and the related costs in the sales department and maintain the same level of sales; or, you could make more effective use of the existing telephone equipment and increase sales. A third alternative would be to take action in both directions, thus getting a double impact on costs. Eliminate the excessive telephone equipment and then make better use of the remaining equipment to increase sales.

Thus a cost improvement can be brought about by avoiding or preventing additional costs while achieving greater productivity; or, the reducing or eliminating of current costs while still achieving the same productivity; or, a combination of both approaches. So, when you evaluate your operations to develop cost improvement opportunities, remember that any change which makes more effective utilization of the company's resources will improve profitability.

Condition Your Thinking

Before digging into the detail evaluation of your operation, put yourself in the right frame of mind. Review again the cost conscious attitude chart. Keep your mind open for all possible opportunities.

Here are some thought provoking statements to think about as you evaluate your operations:

1. It is more important to do the right job than to do the job right.

2. The problem is usually the people who manage costs, not the costs, themselves.
3. Your operations should be results oriented.
4. Strive for effectiveness, not necessarily efficiency.
5. Most cost improvement opportunities will involve other people.
6. Don't try to do more efficiently activities that should not be done at all.
7. Nothing is as easy as it looks.
8. Improvements always mean change, but change does not always mean improvement.
9. There is always an easy solution to every problem. It is generally simple, plausible and wrong!
10. Little improvements can add up to sizeable total dollar savings.

Three Questions to Ask About Every Function

There are no hard and fast rules to follow when you evaluate your operations. Departments and companies vary significantly depending on a whole host of factors. Therefore, the evaluating questions to be discussed in this chapter will have general application and must be adapted to your particular operations. However, three basic questions can be asked of every function:

1. What is being done now that should be done more often?

Examples: More mechanization, competitive bidding on more items, greater employee participation, etc.

2. What is being done now that should be stopped?

Examples: Duplication of functions and activities, unnecessary entertaining, preparation of unneeded reports, etc.

3. What is not being done now that should be?

Examples: Timely order processing, on-time deliveries to customers, investment of idle funds, etc.

Ask these three questions of every function in your operations and the answers will point the way to many cost improvements.

An Overall View of the Evaluation Process

Generally speaking, the operations of any given department can usually be divided into two major categories, those every day *routine operations* which must be performed on an ongoing basis, and the *project type activities* which are based on achieving a specific objective. Dividing your activities into these two categories simplifies evaluation of them as to their effectiveness and enables you to apply specific evaluation techniques to each. It should be kept in mind that the effectiveness of an activity often depends upon the validity of the activity's objective. If the objectives are unsound, then the activity is probably ineffective. No job in a department has meaning unless it moves the department and the company toward its overall objectives. You must first evaluate a department's basic objectives to determine if they are contributing to overall effectiveness.

Once the department's objectives have been evaluated, the manager can evaluate the policies and procedures being followed as well as the activities taking place to achieve those objectives. Ask the question, "Do the current policies and procedures accomplish the overall purpose of the departmental function?" Next, the manager must evaluate the design of the organization. This requires looking at the number and kinds of positions, along with their corresponding duties and responsibilities. An effort should also be made to evaluate any standards which may have been set for the measurement of the level of individual or group performance in completing the department's activities.

Salaries and directly related fringe benefits often represent the major cost in many departments. This is a significant cost of human resources and highlights the need for the manager to do the best possible job in evaluating what people are doing in order to achieve maximum effectiveness with a minimum of staff. The manager should design his organization around the activities which must be performed, not the people who now work in his department.

Dividing Activities Into Evaluation Categories

It is generally easier to evaluate the benefits derived from the various activities if they are separated into some broad evaluation categories. For example, try to separate the various activities into four categories; productive, support, policing and unnecessary.

Productive Type Activities are those which can be related directly to the process of selling, manufacturing, and delivering the product to the customer. These are profit-earning activities and generally add value to the product. Examples of these are: direct sales activities which bring the product to the customer's attention, direct manufacturing activities which produce the product, packing and delivery activities which get the product to the customer.

Productive activities should be evaluated on the basis of productivity. Compare the cost of the activity to the value being added to the product. For instance, direct selling activities are usually classified as operating expenses. Nevertheless, they should be evaluated on the results they produce in terms of volume, margins and other similar criterion. The resources being utilized in productive activities should be concentrated on the products which have the best margins; production facilities should be utilized to produce the more profitable items, etc. From the standpoint of improving profitability it may be advantageous to recommend increasing costs in these areas of activity if it will produce greater volume and additional profits.

The next category is *support type activities*. These are activities which must be carried on in order to support the productive activities, even though they are not directly related to production and sale of the product. Examples of these are: Advertising and Market Research to support the salesmen; Purchasing, Personnel, and Maintenance activities at the plant; Billing and Collecting receivables for the product sold. Support activities are more difficult to evaluate. As a result they often have built-in excesses, which can be a fruitful area for developing cost improvements.

Support activities should first have to prove that they are needed at all. The manager should ask the question, "How much do we stand to lose if we don't perform this function or activity?" There is little point in trying to do efficiently what should not be done at all. If the support function or activity cannot be eliminated, then the next question, "What is the least cost and effort we can get by with and still accomplish our overall objectives?"

The third category is *policing activities*. These activities are aimed at preventing the wrong thing from happening. It's surprising how often you find people checking out someone else's work even when it is not part of the company's formal procedure, when they should be learning to work together and depend upon each other.

Another "hang-up" people seem to have is the checking of work done by computers. Data processed by computers must be controlled but usually simple testing of totals is adequate. How many times have you seen clerks adding up computer runs to make sure that the computer can add. It is amazing sometimes how much time is wasted in this area.

Shop inspection activities and office paperwork audits of various kinds are examples of policing activities which may be far more costly to perform than the cost of the possible mistake they are trying to prevent.

The fourth category is what I term *unnecessary activities*. These are activities which no longer contribute to the objectives of the operation or duplicate other activities. For example, systems may have been mechanized to produce information which is still being manually gathered elsewhere. The objectives of a function change with the passage of time, but often unnecessary activities within the function continue. Obviously they should be eliminated as expeditiously as possible.

Question Everything

The first thing you must learn is to question. As you evaluate the activities of your department, ask "why" constantly. Don't accept stock answers like, "We have always done it that way," "It's company policy," "It can't be done." The cost conscious manager questions everything and has to satisfy himself that every activity has a valid purpose which is producing a benefit for the company.

Costs must first be evaluated to determine why they are incurred and then evaluated to ascertain the benefit they provide is adequate. If possible, try to quantify the benefit so that it can be easily compared to the total cost. Even if you have to estimate the value of the benefits, you should try to put dollar value on them. Let me repeat, *costs should not be incurred unless they provide, either directly or indirectly, a benefit of value to the business.* Costs which are incurred and do not provide a concrete benefit to the business amount to simple waste and should be eliminated as soon as they are identified.

There are areas of operations so small that few people consider them targets for cost improvements, possibly because they feel the potential savings would be unimportant. Don't overlook these small activity areas. Often big savings can result from small problems. Study them and you will find they have a way of adding up, especially if they occur many times a year.

A controller at a large industrial complex noted one plant, though very small, was beyond a doubt the most profitable. One day, during lunch with the plant manager, he asked him this question, "Jake, how is it that your people keep developing so many profit improvement ideas?"

"It's because we think small," he answered. "You are always spreading the philosophy of thinking big, but at our plant nothing is very big so we tell our people to think small. When we save a penny a pound on material it doesn't sound like much, but with our volume use of certain items, it can add up to many thousands of dollars by the end of the year."

That is something to remember. Although "Think Big" and look for those major cost improvements is still good advice, don't forget to look for the little ones as well. They can add up to something big in the long run. Don't let an opportunity get by you. Jot it down for future reference when you see it. You probably will want to concentrate on the big costs first, but later go back and take a look at the smaller ones. Write down every possible cost improvement opportunity, idea or thought, and don't stop asking questions until you are sure you have evaluated every activity. Then go back and start again. You probably missed about half the opportunities the first time.

Challenge Every Activity

A major reason managers don't fully exploit potential cost improvement opportunity areas is because they have accepted without challenge certain practices and procedures which were originated in the past under prior managers. Question every cost incurring activity. Make it prove that its continuation is warranted.

Generally, costs can be reduced by as much as 20% without decreasing the effectiveness of operations in even well-managed businesses. In others not as well managed, substantially greater opportunities exist.

Many books on cost reduction elaborate ways to get your employees to work harder. Working harder may improve results, but working "smarter" is what really counts. This book tries to help the operating manager understand the principles of Managing Costs by offering suggestions and example questions which will help him discover potential opportunity areas where working "smarter" can dynamically increase profits. The questions are purposely worded to help him and his employees challenge current operations. They are only examples to stimulate the manager's thinking about his own operations. Obviously, a list of potential cost improvement questions could never be complete since new methods, processes, and equipment are being introduced daily. Use the examples which can be applied to your operations as a starter list. Add to it every time you discover a new improvement idea. Remember, improvement ideas can come from any employee or outsider.

General Questions to Ask
When You Evaluate Your Operations

In conducting a cost management review of a department or company, a list of questions can be a great aid to assure coverage of all the major cost generating areas. It's also a help to the manager in organizing his thinking and conclusions. Such a list varies from department to department depending on the functions being examined, but some questions are common to all departments.

The following chapters outline a number of questions which have stimulated cost improvements. You should not limit your questions to those presented here. These examples are given only to provide a framework for you to develop your own approach. Simply following this list as you would a checklist would make your review too rigid and unimaginative. Each department's methods of operation are different and many questions which would pertain to a particular function of one would not apply to another. With this warning, let's look at some sample questions which may help you evaluate the operations of your department or company.

1. *Have you defined your department's goals in writing?* As manager of a department you must know what you are trying to accomplish. Committing your objectives in writing is the first step to evaluating the validity of those goals. The simple act of putting your objectives down on paper helps to organize your thinking.

2. *Are the stated objectives for your department understood by your subordinates?* Cost Management requires getting results through the people you manage. You, the manager, cannot do it alone. Therefore, do everything you can to let each of your subordinates participate in your cost management program. To get their fullest help and cooperation they must understand what you are trying to accomplish. Get them involved at the beginning when you are evaluating the objectives of your department.

3. *Do you, as the manager of the department, have*

access to the financial information you need to control costs properly and to administer your department? How effective is the information you have to manage your costs? Do you understand and use it? How could it be improved? Does your financial reporting system provide for adequate expense control procedures? Cost information reports and cost management are inseparable. Review the types of reports you are now getting from your financial department. Are they structured to show departmental or unit responsibility for various operations? Do the reports include comparisons of costs to budgeted or standard allowances? Are sales forecasts and projections of working capital investments also compared to actual results? Did you as the manager participate in preparing the forecasts or was it prepared by the accounting department or higher management? Do the procedures require forecasting of capital assets to be acquired during the forecast period? Are appropriations with justification data required and approved before fixed assets are acquired? If your operations use standard costs for comparing results, are those standard costs close to actual? If not, your performance comparison could be materially distorted. Are your operations or the company's products periodically evaluated by break-even chart analysis? Do the break-even charts properly reflect fixed and variable costs? Are financial reports showing actual results utilized in wage administration, i.e., job evaluation and merit ratings? Are the financial reports simply historical information rather than management and action oriented?

These are only a few examples of questions you might ask about the cost management information available to you. If you are not receiving adequate information to evaluate your operations you must insist that it be provided. It is surprising how many managers just assume they must work with what they have rather than ask for what they need. Discuss your requirements with your controller or accounting manager. He may already have the information available but does not issue it because no one has asked for it before. Keep in mind that his accounting system is structured to provide information to many types of different users.

In many companies segments of the business are segregated and put under the operational control of different individuals who are specialists for that particular activity. Generally, the financial structure of the company's accounting and reporting system is geared to coincide with the operational structure, in order to have financial reporting on an operational basis. The financial reporting structure must also serve as a vehicle for accumulation of costs which will fairly reflect individual products and show the true total costs of each function. In any accounting system there are compromises to achieve maximum effectiveness without keeping several sets of accounting records. In your company the accounting system probably serves many purposes as follows:

a. Financial reporting for stockholders, financial institutions, and the general public's review of your company operations. The accounting profession, Securities and Exchange Commission, as well as the general public, have generated the ground rules, the accepted principles, which dictate the manner in which the records of the company must be kept for this purpose.

b. Financial reporting for tax purposes is in many cases different than that of reporting for the general public's review. Tax accounting rules have been developed by statute through the many government bodies, both State and Federal, and often-times have little, if any sound logic from a business standpoint. Most individuals think of tax accounting rules as applying only to income tax considerations since they are familiar with their annual task of preparing their own individual tax return. However, in business there are also the problems associated with payroll taxes, sales and use taxes, franchise taxes, etc. So the accounting system must recognize the needs of the many different tax reports that are issued periodically. For example, different types of supplies and materials are sometimes taxed at different use tax rates.

c. The most important requirement of the financial reporting system is to serve management. To tell the story
   of the company's operations as it really is, in order to
   give you, the manager, the information you need to
   make the daily decisions necessary to control your
   operations. However, when I say "manager" just what
   manager am I talking about? The Corporate manager's
   need for overall information to make decisions regarding overall financing, etc., is somewhat different from
   a plant manager's needs.

   Different plant managers have different ideas as to
   what is proper from an accounting standpoint, especially when the profit results are the means by which their
   individual plant's operations are measured. The same
   situation occurs at the department levels. At the foreman level, with the many backgrounds and preconceived ideas of what the accounting system should do
   or not do, the problem becomes immense.

d. Your company's financial reporting system must also
   serve to allocate costs by product line. This facilitates
   pricing decisions and evaluation of products.

e. The reporting system must also break down costs by
   function or activity. This allows analysis of the effectiveness of individual operations and is used in evaluating
   new methods, make or buy decisions, etc.

f. Government contracting offices also have developed
   their own accounting principles which must be taken
   into consideration when a company is working on government contracts.

It's obvious that companies have a choice of maintaining several different accounting records, all of which would
give different answers, and thus would be suspect by each
user group, or of maintaining one overall system, which
with appropriate compromises will satisfy all groups. Such
an overall system requires a great deal more detail break-

down of costs than would be necessary if the system had to serve only one of the above requirements.

To add to the confusion of your company's accounting and reporting system, most of the user groups have an army of individuals called "auditors." The Board of Directors, acting on behalf of the stockholders and general public, hires an outside public accounting firm to test the records and submit their opinion as to the fairness of the reporting system. Many Corporate headquarters have groups of internal auditors who are constantly testing to see that the accounting system provides fiscal protection for the company's assets. The Internal Revenue Service has auditors to see that income tax and payroll tax reporting is in accordance with their rules. The State Sales Tax Departments (50 states) each have audit groups, and the list could go on and on.

Your company's present reporting system, although it is complex, is a system that has developed out of the thoughts and influence of many individuals. As we have said, discuss your needs with your controller or accounting manager. His department has a wealth of information which can usually be made available to suit your requirements.

4. *Is there a written manual that covers at least the routine procedures of your department?* No matter how varied your department's functions may be there are usually some aspects of it which are repetitive and therefore lend themselves to written description. Written procedures are extremely helpful in evaluating needed changes; also they save substantial loss in efficiency when new employees are trained.

5. *Do you as the manager of your department allow your key employees to develop their own cost improvement ideas and then allow them to implement those improvements within their area of responsibility?* If a manager never really delegates authority to his supervisors and in-

sists on participating in every decision, it's pretty difficult to install a cost management approach which provides for recognizing people based on their own achievements. Unless employees at all levels are made to feel that they are working in an environment which allows them to contribute, they will soon cease to contribute. If a manager stifles that spirit by always having the last word, or by constantly insisting on converting his subordinates' ideas to his own way of thinking, he will soon find that his operation's potential is limited to his own abilities. Don't limit your cost improvement potential. Encourage your employees' participation. This is a sought after, highly valuable resource. Let your employees get as much recognition from every idea as possible.

Often the major benefit a cost improvement idea brings is the "job enrichment" it offers as a reward to its creator. The "idea man" is one of the most valuable employees a company possesses. Solutions to problems, strategies which defeat competition, marketing concepts which increase sales, new methods which improve effectiveness and the economics which improve costs and profits—mostly all emanate from his proposals.

Whether a manager provides monetary rewards to the employee or not, cost conscious people like the excitement of developing new and better ways of doing things. When others show a favorable response to their concept and their ideas are implemented and recognized by others there's a deep sense of accomplishment.

6. *Do you have a system for updating your department's policy and procedure manuals when changes occur?* Most policies and procedures are obsolete within a few years. They must change to cope with the everchanging government regulations, economic conditions, size of the business, etc. Unless a system exists to keep written manuals up-to-date they quickly become useless.

Many companies have typewriters which can store data on magnetic tape or cards, subject to later recall for making changes. However, someone must be assigned the duty of reporting the changes and issuing revisions.

7. *Have you and your employees identified the priority of your goals and do you adhere to those priorities once they are set?* Many departments are so busy putting out today's "fires" there isn't time to solve the big problems, much less to tackle the major opportunity areas within their responsibility. Setting priorities is first a matter of attitude and second, one of approach. Successful managers have a "priority attitude." They tackle the major problems first and let the little ones be handled as they go along. Other managers take an opposite approach. They attempt to get all the little problems out of the way before getting to the big ones. However, all the "little ones" use up their time and the main opportunities are never exploited.

An example of this priority attitude: There was a small plant manager who was understaffed but, nevertheless, was always able to produce and ship a quality product on schedule and at a good profit margin. Because he was short of help, he occasionally neglected to submit all the reports which the home office requested. He intentionally directed his efforts toward those tasks which directly affected the profit of the plant. Necessary reporting of his operations was limited to action type reports that stated the facts with limited embellishment.

Too often in large companies this type of manager is not known for the profits he contributes but rather as the one who doesn't supply his reports on time. Sometimes he becomes frustrated with the Corporate management who continually badger him with more requests for information and leaves the company. He is then replaced by a hard working but inexperienced man. Corporate staff members impress upon him the problem of preparing detail reports on the operation. As a result the new manager devotes his major attention to increasing the quantity of data furnished. The understaffed problem is solved by adding people. Then someone notices that profit margins are not as good as before. More reports are requested: more staff is added, even perhaps a computer. Before anyone realizes what is happening, the company has suffered a severe blow to profits.

Is the example exaggerated? Not really. Managers at all levels have been known to focus their attention in reverse priority. Be sure you identify the right order of priority. Recognize the importance of developing a "priority attitude" for yourself and your employees. Then utilize your stated objectives to determine what your department's priorities are and whether or not they are being neglected. If you have difficulty with the home office, try to convince them to adopt a "priority attitude" and judge your performance on results instead of the volume of paper. The activities of your department can generally be sorted out into three priority categories:

1. One high priority group where, with a little more effort, extraordinary results can be achieved.

2. One high priority group where rapid and purposeful elimination of the activity is indicated.

3. One large and heterogeneous group of activities which require detail evaluation or major changes to produce significant improvements.

When a manager and his people look at their operations using these priority categories, a list of major opportunity areas will begin to emerge. This list can be used as the framework for beginning your cost management efforts. Dynamically quick profit improvements can often be obtained by exploiting the first two major opportunity categories. Resources should first be allocated to these high priority opportunity areas to produce dynamic results.

8. *Is there an obvious imbalance of the work load in your department?* Is this a result of poor organization or failure of you and your supervisors to distribute the work evenly? Temporary imbalances of the work flow often result from seasonal fluctuations. Allowed to remain out

of balance, they can seriously affect the morale and effectiveness of your operations.

Proper balance of work load, especially urgent task assignments, is most important to get work done promptly and efficiently. Review your organization and the activities within each group. Which activities take the most time? Is the largest amount of time being spent on the major activity in your department? If not, find out why. Are you using your people's skill properly and to maximum advantage? If your employees are working above or below their ability levels, then you are misusing your manpower resources. Productivity, work quality, and morale usually suffer as a result.

Are work assignments spread too thin? Is responsibility for the various activities too decentralized? Employees get greater job satisfaction from seeing a job through to completion. Effort can also be saved if jobs are done by fewer people.

Are there misdirected efforts? Perhaps closer supervision or retraining are needed to prevent too much time being devoted to relatively unimportant tasks. All of these problems which hinder effectiveness can be identified with a staffing review similar to the example discussed in Chapter 4. Use it to get the facts and then restructure your department's organization and work loads to improve the cost effectiveness of your operations.

9. *Is there an atmosphere within your department conducive to open, frank exchange of opinion or is there an air of secrecy which pervades so that employees are uncomfortable discussing their jobs, company policy or your internal procedures?* Many managers create a barrier between themselves and their employees by not providing time to listen to their employees. Don't just listen when the employee is talking about the specific job or task he is working at. Be ready to listen to his personal problems as well. Let your "hair down" and get to know your people as individuals. Whenever employees feel that their thoughts

don't matter because no one listens anyway, department morale suffers. Keep in mind that your people are more likely to know the problems and opportunity areas in the department than you are. Encourage them to speak out. Invite their frank opinion about your internal policies and procedures. Communication in a company should travel both ways. Don't restrict the upward flow of ideas.

10. *Are top management and yourself genuinely interested in developing cost improvements or are you and they too busy at other things to give the attention required?* Cost Management will be more effective if it is enthusiastically endorsed by top management. Laxity on their part permeates the entire organization. Therefore, you, the manager of your department, must participate fully in the development and implementation of cost improvement projects. Your subordinates will respond and take it seriously only to the extent that they feel you are behind it. Many competent managers are cost conscious themselves but fail to communicate this attitude to their subordinates. Employees cannot be motivated until they understand it is one of your major concerns. Meet with your people in small groups or call a meeting of your entire department. Give them the facts and explain what you are trying to do. Ask for their help. But remember, actions speak louder than words. A long discussion about the need to reduce expenses will have little effect if the manager then proceeds to redecorate his office, spend his time on the golf course, or exhibits other behavior which in the eyes of his employees represents a lack of attention to cost control.

11. *Does your company have a way for all employees to submit their cost improvement ideas?* For cost management to be effective a constant flow of ideas is required. Suggestion systems which offer personal incentives to employees can provide management with a valuable source of cost improvement ideas. To be most effective the employee should be notified in writing as soon as possible regarding the disposition of his idea. If accepted the incen-

tive should be paid promptly. If rejected he should be told why. Employee participation in the implementation of the cost improvement should be encouraged where practical. Suggestion plans which lack the above requirements soon die from lack of participation. The incentive need not be large. In most cases employees participate in order to gain recognition, but small cash payments or gifts foster greater participation and boost employee morale.

If your company doesn't already have a suggestion system, why not introduce one. If your company has one now, encourage your subordinates to participate and then utilize their suggestions wherever practical.

12. *Is there duplication among departments?* It is surprising how much duplication there is among departments and activities. Many times this is caused by the lack of understanding among the managers regarding the operations of each other's departments. Unless someone looks at the company's various activities on an overall objective basis, these duplications can go on for long periods of time.

The Cost Management Review discussed in Chapter 4 can be very helpful in identifying duplications in detail activities if made on a company-wide basis. Joint staff meetings, where each manager describes his operations to the others, can also be useful in eliminating duplicated activities. Eliminating duplication among the various operations is easy once identified and should be a goal of every manager.

13. *How much effort is being utilized for policing type activities?* Reduce to a minium those functions whose sole duty is to police other departments. Concentrate on training available staff to do the job right in the first place. Build internal controls into the procedures which spotlight errors and exceptions. Utilize exception reports to notify management of major variations from accepted practice. Examine all policing type activities to determine if they are needed, and decide on the minimum.

14. *How often do you make comparisons of the number*

of personnel on the payroll between periods? Have you studied employment and rate statistics? Staffing in departments can grow rapidly if not constantly reviewed. Managers should be able to justify each and every employee who reports to them. If you find staffing increasing, compare the additional cost with the additional benefits to the company. Managers often feel that their importance in the organization is related to the number of people under their supervision. Discourage that kind of thinking. Point out that it is results that count.

15. *What approvals are required to add personnel?* Adding staff to cover an increased work load is easy. Developing ways to complete the additional work without increasing staff is more difficult. Many managers will take the easy way. Requiring higher approval for hiring staff, even replacements, provides an objective second look at the actual need.

16. *When mistakes are made, are they investigated as to why they occurred and the needed corrective measures?* Mistakes often indicate problems, and problems often point to improvement opportunities. We can learn from our mistakes if we approach them with a mature attitude. A manager who is too critical of his employees when mistakes are made discourages them from doing any creative thinking, or from trying anything different. Managers who investigate errors, try to understand why they happened and then work with the employees to prevent the same thing from happening in the future will find their department growing into a dynamic, innovative, problem solving unit.

17. *Do you and your employees spend too much of your time correcting situations that should not have been allowed to arise in the first place?* Do you find yourself anticipating problems or are you simply reacting when they occur? The best way to handle a problem is to prevent it. If the same situation keeps recurring, find out why and develop ways to prevent it in the future.

Problems seem to occur just when you are busiest. Many managers simply do whatever is necessary to clear up the situation for the moment. They don't take the time to see what can be done to prevent its happening again. When the problem occurs is when all the facts are fresh in everybody's mind. Take enough time at least to get the facts while they are available, even though time does not permit a complete solution. You will have the information stored in your mind where your subconscious can be working on the problem. Then when you think of a long term solution, it will probably be a good one because you were able to start working on it before the problem recurred.

18. *Is your department still beset by any problems that were identified previously and brought to the attention of top management?* Many times a problem requires a solution which needs the assistance of other departments or higher management for implementation. Simply "passing the buck" by referring it to higher management and using their non-attention as an excuse for not solving the problem is bad management practice. Reconsider how you presented it to higher management? Did you properly emphasize the cost impact on your operations? Was its solution really the responsibility of someone else or could much of it actually have been solved within your own jurisdiction? Have you made any attempt on your own to solicit the help of another involved department? As long as the problem is affecting your operations' profitability, it is up to you to get something done about it. Re-evaluate both the problem and your proposed solution. Then go out and solicit the help you need to solve it.

19. *Do you as a department manager set aside specific time to plan and review the activities of your department?* Think about how you spend your time. How much do you actually spend planning the activities of your department. Planning is probably the most important activity you do, yet many managers neglect this activity more than any other. It has to be an integral part of a manager's

duties or else his department soon loses its direction and effectiveness. Don't let your department become a "planless" operation. Take the time necessary to develop definite strategies and specific programs for accomplishing your objectives. Then, review and monitor your progress. Only through continued review and replanning can you keep your operations headed in the right direction. Don't neglect this major management responsibility.

20. *Does your department's effectiveness depend on the capabilities of one man?* If so, is at least one other person being trained for that critical position? No department should let its future depend solely on the abilities of one man or one group of individuals. Cross train your employees in each other's job. Develop backup for critical positions. Departments which have failed in this development area have eventually regretted it.

21. *Is any portion of the department's work load unessential?* Has the department outlived its purpose? Can its duties be easily assimilated into the routine of another department? This is a tough question for a manager to answer honestly, especially if the entire department has outlived its purpose. Generally, even in organizations where cost management reviews have been limited, entire departments do not become obsolete overnight. New objectives and directions develop and some activities become unessential. Most cost management reviews point out many opportunity areas which add to the department's activities. It is usually a matter of shifting resources from the unessential to the essential. In any event, a manager should answer this question himself before someone in higher management brings the subject up. That way he has time to make the necessary changes to improve his effectiveness before someone else makes his decisions for him.

22. *Do you have a systematic way to review your employees' efficiency and productivity other than your "gut feel," and are those criteria for the review explained and*

universally applied to all employees? It is important that employees not only understand what their duties and objectives are, but also how they will be judged in their success or failure to reach those goals. They need to know how their performance will be measured and that the same standards will be applied to all employees. Favoritism in the form of promotions, merit increases or bonuses, excessive time off, or other "gifts" bestowed by a manager on undeserving employees can wreck morale in any department. It is equally detrimental to use seniority as the only criteria for advancement.

Establish a set of performance standards for all employees. Make sure your employees understand the procedure, and apply it fairly to all. Base your standards on measurable performance indicators which emphasize all the objectives of your department, in proportion to their importance. Tangible forms of recognition can be powerful motivators if properly utilized and can be equally demotivating when misapplied.

23. *Are you as a department manager aware of your budget?* Did you participate in the development of it? Do you feel it is realistic? Is it actually attainable, and are you making conscientious efforts to stay within it?

Manager attitudes were discussed briefly earlier in this book. However some managers still do not participate fully in the preparation of the detail budgets for their operations. They allow higher management to set the monetary goals knowing they are unrealistic. Even where managers do participate in the setting of budget goals, they often submit projected expense levels they feel will be accepted rather than carefully evaluated operational plans of attainable objectives. As a result, they spend a substantial portion of their time projecting what's going to happen and as much or more time explaining why it didn't.

Departmental budgets should be simply your operating plans expressed in dollars and cents—the language of business. They are an excellent tool for planning and controlling your operations. They also facilitate measurement of your effectiveness in achieving your goals.

One of the unique characteristics of departmental budgets, when properly administered is their ability to draw upon the ideas of all the people in your department. By utilizing your key people in its preparation, you incorporate the thinking of those who are close to the everyday problems. A good budget is an effective device to draw out latent ideas, apply psychological incentives, encourage the use of good cost management practices, and develop the managerial skills of your subordinates. Properly conceived, skillfully administered, and imaginatively used, a department budget is a versatile catalytic agent.

Don't fail to plan your budget carefully and assure yourself that its goals are realistic and attainable. Then make a conscientious effort to meet or exceed those goals.

24. *Are your employees aware of the role your department must play in the general scheme of things?* Do they know how the department's contributions affect the end product or overall company objectives? Your employees may fully understand your departmental objectives, but do they understand how those objectives contribute to the end product produced by the company? It is usually reasonably easy for an employee who is directly involved in the production of the company's product to relate his efforts to that end product. However, a typist in the office typing pool or a clerk in the central files department may never have even seen a picture of the end product. Sometimes even production workers are involved with such a small part of the end product that it is difficult for them to visualize how their small segment is important to the whole. It is difficult for them to understand how making small improvements in their job tasks can contribute to the company as a whole.

However, small improvements soon add up to big savings. Keep your employees informed about major achievements of the company. Make them feel a part of those achievements by pointing out wherever possible how their job contributed.

25. *If your department is not accomplishing what it is supposed to, is it's low performance a direct result of a poorly designed organization?* This question can be equally applied to the company as a whole. When was the last time you made a review of your organizational structure? Simplification of an organizational structure may reduce staffing costs. Top-heavy supervision is extremely costly and inefficient. Look for "one-on-one" situations; that is, where a manager has his staff report through one individual. This man in the middle is often excess, unless he is being trained to take over and eliminate the man above him within a short period of time.

Looking at the overall company we find many organizations are too complex and have an excessive number of subsidiaries, divisions, sections and departments. In the past many organizations were made up of several separate corporate entities. This was done in order to take advantage of the multiple "surtax" exemptions for tax purposes. Even though that loophole was eliminated from the IRS code, the complicated corporate structures continued. Also, many companies have acquired other companies and kept inactive corporate entities alive without valid reasons. With the increasing number of government reporting requirements, the cost of maintaining these complicated organizations can become excessive. Review your organization and make sure that every corporate entity in it has a valid reason to be continued. Look at each division and department. Are they all large enough to warrant their own manager or should some be combined for greater efficiency? You may find that some departments or divisions are no longer necessary.

26. *Do you believe you are being given sufficient information to properly administer your department?* If not, what do you believe you need in addition to what you are now receiving? An earlier question referred to financial

data, but there are many other kinds of information a manager needs to run his department effectively. Marketing data, personnel data or production information could be essential to your operation. Make a list of the types of information you feel you need and then find out how to obtain that information. Many times other departments already have what you need, but it has never been asked for before.

27. *If you are receiving enough information, is it accurate, relevant, up-to-date and timely?* Obviously, if it is not, there is little sense in continuing to ask for it. Either it should be discontinued, revised or made useful.

Bring the problem to the attention of the responsible manager. Explain what you need and why. Most managers conscientiously want to improve the information they produce. Simply bringing it to their attention may be all that is needed to improve the situation.

28. *Other Questions:*
   a. Does your department have the authority to order, purchase or otherwise acquire its own supplies? If not, is there a bottleneck in this area that could be avoided if you had such a responsibility?
   b. Is the physical layout of your department conducive to maximum efficiency?
   c. What is the general level of housekeeping performed by your department? Is the office space adequate, clean and properly heated or cooled? Surroundings can have a substantial affect on morale and productivity levels.
   d. Are the security measures taken by your department adequate protection against loss from fire or theft?
   e. Do you and your employees have a cooperative attitude toward other departments?
   f. Do you, the manager, make an effort to learn what the department turnover rate, absentee rate, and morale level are? Do you compare them with those of the rest of the company or other departments?

Excessive employee turnover can increase costs substantially.

There are many more questions you should ask about your operations. Space does not permit more examples here. Use the examples given as a starting point only. Then add others which are applicable to your industry or type of business. In later chapters we will discuss more questions about specific operating costs, but first let's look at an area of cost management which is often overlooked by managers.

6 MANAGING ASSETS FOR PROFIT IMPROVEMENT

Many managers do not think of working capital and fixed assets as areas for development of cost management opportunities. Yet, businesses borrow money to help finance these assets and must pay interest on this borrowed capital. This interest cost could be significant. Attempts to reduce it must focus on the manager's ability to maintain asset investment at levels which minimize financing costs yet do not limit the company's potential and growth. Any book on increasing profits by managing costs would not be complete unless we explored possible ways of reducing our investment in Fixed Assets and Working Capital.

This chapter outlines a number of questions to stimulate reduced investment and related cost. Reviewing these investment areas will also stimulate other cost improvement ideas. It should be stressed that these examples provide only a framework upon which to develop your own approach.

Cash

1. *Do you maintain cash balances in excess of your base requirements?* Large companies pursue opportunities to utilize their cash assets with greater zeal than they pursue opportunities to increase profits. They have cash man-

agers who devote all their time to developing innovative ways to keep every dollar working. Medium and smaller companies overlook these opportunities because the amounts seem small. They fail to see that any balance which stands idle could be a contributor to profits if properly utilized. Some cash is needed in a checking account to cover service charges for the work performed by the respective banking institutions. However, seasonal fluctuations can cause excess cash funds during certain periods. Anything in excess of your base requirements is wasting assets. Discuss it with your banker. Based on the activity in your account, he will be able to tell you what is actually needed. The difference can be invested in short term government securities or other opportunities.

Shop around. Banks have different ways of computing your minimum balance requirements. It's possible another bank could make a substantial reduction in your cash requirement. Invest the difference and add income to your operations.

2. *Does your company maintain too many bank accounts?* It is possible to operate segments of a company with no bank account. Sometimes with one account, and usually with no more than two. If you are maintaining more, question why. Substantial savings in accounting effort can be realized by minimizing the number of bank accounts.

3. *Have you considered using zero balance accounts?* Some companies have good reason to maintain several bank accounts; such as, separate accounts for subsidiary operations, payroll, collections, etc. If this is so in your company, you might find the use of zero balance accounts advantageous for keeping cash balances at a minimum.

When you use this approach, as many accounts as possible are maintained in a single bank. One master account is maintained with a balance sufficient to cover the activity in all accounts while all the other accounts have a zero balance. Each day the bank totals the checks which clear each account and automatically transfers sufficient funds to each of the zero balance accounts to cover the checks which clear that day. Any excess cash over the amount required by the bank as a minimum balance to cover the activity in all the accounts is thus consolidated and available for short term investment. Automatic transfer from collection accounts can also be arranged.

4. *Are you getting maximum use from borrowed capital?* The advantages and economics of borrowed capital versus equity capital should be evaluated carefully. The principle of using other people's money (OPM) can dramatically affect the return on investment (ROI). The interest cost for loans should be studied in detail, however. Obtaining the right balance between borrowed capital and stockholder investment is a subject by itself. Space does not permit more than a mention of it here. If your company is passing up significant returns because of lack of funds, a complete study of your company's financial status could prove extremely profitable. Many banks have officers who are experts in the field. They can assist you in determining the best approach for your particular business.

5. *Are you paying out too much in dividends?* Your dividend policies may not be recognizing the capital requirements of the company. Financial statements are based on the historical cost of fixed assets. Companies who acquired assets several years ago and charge depreciation based on those costs may be showing "phantom" profits in relation to the cost of replacement today. An example of this is the nation's railroads which reported substantial profits and paid dividends thereon for many years while their equipment grew older each year. When they finally recognized the need to make major replacements at current equipment costs, they were faced with a major financial problem.

Smaller businesses may be following a similar shortsighted approach. What would the real profits of your business be if you calculated your depreciation based on current replacement costs? If your company hasn't studied this effect of inflation, it should. The results of such a study might shock you.

6. *Do you use all the bank services you should?* Many banks can provide extra services such as payroll preparation, reconciliation of accounts, and freight bill payments at less cost to you than your present procedure. Even companies which have centralized computer installations have found that their diversified locations can benefit by using local bank processing facilities for specialized applications such as payrolls and freight payments. Your banker can give you all the information you need to evaluate the cost effectiveness of such arrangements.

Accounts Receivable

1. *Is too much of your capital tied up in Accounts Receivable?* Faster turnover can be obtained by *selling* accounts receivable. Most businessmen think that turning their receivables over as security for loans is an arrangement used only by companies which are in financial trouble. However, if that capital can be reinvested in your business to earn a return greater than the interest charges, it makes good sense to evaluate the possibilities.

With the many bank charge plans such as "Master Charge" and "BankAmericard," many consumer oriented businesses have virtually eliminated accounts receivable. The discount charged by banks for collecting your receivables under these plans is often less than the cost of keeping customer accounts on your books, sending out statements, and following up to assure final collection, especially if small amounts are involved.

2. *How effective are your accounts receivable credit and collection procedures?* Large past due accounts might indicate loose credit policies or failure to follow-up on collections. In times of tight money smart financial men delay payment of money owed to the last possible moment. Your

customers may delay payment to you beyond your normal credit terms. Many customers will take as much additional time as you allow. Failure to follow-up on slow paying accounts can cost you significant amounts in terms of additional investment in receivables.

Many companies now charge 12% to 18% interest on accounts which are not paid when due. Others have added a percentage to their selling price and then give it back as a discount for quicker payment. Make a review of your credit policies and collection follow-up procedures. An improvement in this area could reduce your working capital investment in receivables, and possibly could add interest income to your profits.

3. *Are you issuing too many credit memos on accounts receivable?* Preparation of credit memoranda is quite costly. Minimization of this unnecessary expense can be accomplished by locating the source of the error—pricing, shipping, order writing, clerical errors, etc. Too many errors can also affect your image with customers and delay receipt of accounts receivable payments.

A review of this area may also point out other problems which need correcting such as; inadequate packing which is causing excessive breakage in shipment, salesmen quoting wrong prices, (Customers usually complain about errors in your favor. What about errors that go the other way?), and over and undershipment, with the credits being issued only for undershipments.

Credit memos are often accompanied by customer complaints. Unless credits are being approved by someone high enough in the organization, perhaps unwarranted credits are being issued. A careful review in this area can identify many cost improvement opportunities.

4. *Do your customers take cash discounts after the allowable period?* Some companies are quite meticulous in following up on unearned discounts regardless of the expense involved. Writing letters and making telephone calls to collect minor amounts is "Pennywise and Pound

Foolish." A minimum amount should be established for follow-up. The time spent on chasing small discount amounts is better used following up delinquent accounts.

5. *How timely is your order processing function?* A comparison of order and shipment dates may reflect an excessive order processing cycle. Often sales and profits are lost because of long lead times between placement of the customer's order and the date he receives the product. Customers who can't wait may buy from a competitor instead. These lead times could be dependent upon how busy the production facility is when an order is received. However, some companies find that order processing and related paperwork flow cause a substantial delay in the overall cycle.

Review the time it takes a customer's order to reach the production department. Delays in order processing can represent a substantial percent of the total cycle.

6. *Is credit approval delaying your order processing?* Eliminate order-by-order credit approval for customers whose credit ratings are beyond question. Establish credit limits for repeat customers. This speeds up order processing with consequent savings in paper handling costs.

Some companies have found they can parallel the credit approval procedure with the order processing or production cycle. The goods can then be held for shipment until credit approval is final. Where custom products are involved, a deposit sufficient to cover the initial period required for approval is requested from new accounts. All of these methods reduce order processing time with minimal risk and help to improve "lead times" for customers.

7. *How do you provide for uncollectible accounts receivable?* Immediate cash savings may be achieved in deferred taxes by changing from a "charge-off" basis to a reserve method for uncollectible accounts. If you presently charge off bad debts when they become uncollectible, it is possible to elect a change in accounting method for

income tax purposes. Start setting up a reserve for expected losses based on your past experience. The reserve for uncollectible receivables thus becomes a tax deductible item.

Inventories

1. *Are your operations affected by seasonal fluctuations?* In businesses with seasonal characteristics stabilizing production throughout the year may result in more efficient utilization of personnel and facilities. Many times this requires building up inventories during slow periods for shipment during the peak periods. So, be sure to take into account the cost of carrying those higher inventories when you evaluate the potential savings.

Stabilizing production this way requires good sales forecasting. If your forecasting has been weak in the past, exercise care and improve your forecasting techniques first. Otherwise you could find yourself with excess or even obsolete inventories which could quickly offset any cost savings gained in leveling production.

Sometimes companies are able to coordinate seasonal fluctuations with customer's advance orders and extended payment terms. By shipping ahead of schedule to customers and offering delayed payment, you move inventories into a receivable category. This becomes better collateral for loans and it also eliminates the cost of storing finished goods for later shipments. Warehousing costs can run to 25% for handling, space, breakage, obsolescence, etc. Shipping the products to customers eliminates these costs. Forecasting of actual shipment is of course more accurate if you have firm orders from customers.

2. *Do you have slow moving or obsolete items in your inventories?* A review of causes for high obsolete and surplus inventory often discloses: (a) poor purchasing policies; (b) inadequate material, inventory and production control procedures; (c) improper sales forecasting; or (d) excessive engineering changes in designs and specifications. Improvements in any one or all of these critical inventory

control areas can result in substantial profit increases. Obsolete or slow moving inventories not only cost money to keep on hand, but eventually result in write-offs, or at best disposal at distressed prices. They also tie up valuable working capital which is no longer working for you.

Start by taking a hard look at your purchasing procedures. Weak purchasing policies and procedures are often the major cause of excess and obsolete inventories. The purchasing department can have a great influence on many costs, and inventory levels particularly. Because of its close relationship with vendors and other purchasing agents it is also in the best position to help dispose of excess inventories, through returning them to the appropriate vendor or finding other companies who can use the items. Make a list of the problem items. Then go to the purchasing department and determine first why the item was purchased; and, then what can be done to keep excess and obsolete items to a minimum in the future.

Next, review your inventory control procedures. Are inventory quantities regularly compared to expected future usage? When excess quantities are first noted, who is notified and is any action taken? Early identification followed by quick action can minimize loss from obsolete or slow moving inventory items. Inventory problems of this type seldom improve with the passage of time.

Perhaps optimistic sales forecasts have caused items to become overstocked. When revisions are made in sales projections, does anyone make a simultaneous review of inventory balances and purchase or production orders which have been placed? There may still be time to cancel or defer orders which would increase inventory levels.

What about engineering changes? Before they are made are plans formulated to utilize inventory on hand which will become obsolete by the change? Are amounts on order considered in these plans? Engineering changes are often made to reduce the cost of the product. However, unless careful plans are implemented to use up the existing inventory, the cost of the old obsolete items can offset much of the expected savings. Make sure that both inventory management and purchasing personnel are made immediately aware of engineering changes to minimize inventory losses of this type.

3. *What steps are taken to dispose of excess or obsolete inventories?* Obsolete and surplus inventory items create additional storage and handling costs. It also ties up working capital. Unfortunately, some managers tend to procrastinate when it becomes evident that an inventory loss should be recognized. The problem gets worse with the passage of time. Some managers like to wait for a better than average month in which to take the write-off and dispose of the items. What they fail to realize is that the carrying costs (storage space, handling, investment of the recovery value) tend to work against them and the amount of recovery value will probably be less in the end.

4. *How many different inventory records are maintained?* Duplication of perpetual records in the stores, production control, purchasing and cost accounting departments is quite common, and often they all have different balances. Many companies could substantially improve their control over inventories if they would maintain one highly accurate system, rather than several partial sets of records.

Since each of the groups requires different types of information about inventory status, they feel the necessity to maintain separate records to cater to their requirements. The updating of perpetual records is often only a part-time activity and the job is not done on a timely and accurate basis. It is not unusual in such a situation to find the various groups constantly in disagreement over the status of inventory information. Each group is basing its decisions on somewhat different information and it is therefore difficult to function smoothly as a team. By developing and installing one overall inventory information system which satisfies the requirements of all groups, it is often possible to achieve a significant cost improvement and substantially improve the operations of all departments.

5. *Is the ABC method of inventory control used?* This method focuses management attention toward the 20% of the inventory which usually represents 80% of the investment.

"A" items, those having high dollar value, should be closely controlled with perpetual records and constant requirement review. Minimum effort here can produce major results.

"B" items, medium dollar value, should be investigated as to degree of control required. Depending on your particular business, these items require less attention usually.

"C" items, inexpensive and numerous, can be controlled with minimum records, or expensed as purchased since they represent such a low percentage of cost. Perpetual records and general ledger controls may be completely eliminated for these inventories of minor value with high activity.

If you have not utilized this ABC technique of focusing both management attention and control efforts in the past, examine it thoroughly. You will find that with the same, or less, cost for record keeping and control you can achieve both inventory reductions and improved control over inventories.

6. *Have you looked at specific categories of inventories?* A large number of *raw materials* of similar specifications with varying sizes may indicate a need for procedures to establish standard material specifications. Coordination of engineering, production, and purchasing in setting material standards can have a tremendous impact on inventory levels and result in clerical savings throughout the organization.

Finished stock inventories are often needlessly composed of an excessive number of items with similar specifications. Sales departments may not know the benefits of maximum standardization. Segregation and classification of *scrap* inventories by type and size, etc., can result in greater recovery.

Other Current Assets

1. *Have you reviewed other assets for improvement opportunities?* These items are usually minor but a few minutes review can turn up significant improvement opportunities. Many companies for example defer once-a-year type payments and then write them off over the remaining periods in the year. Expensing small items as incurred eliminates the need for this monthly amortization and results in significant clerical savings with little or no distortion in departmental operations.

Prepaid insurance can lead you to savings opportunities. Review your insurance program on a competitive basis and look for reduced premiums with satisfactory coverage. Rates for fire insurance are based on conditions in your particular operation. Minimizing fire hazards reduces premiums. Rates for workmen's compensation insurance fluctuate with experience. Analyze past accidents and eliminate unsafe physical conditions and hazardous practices.

Fixed Assets

1. *Are your plant and equipment fully depreciated?* Although a large amount of fully depreciated equipment may be an advantage, it may also indicate that product costs are not realistic because true depreciation is not recognized. Operations may be inefficient because of worn out equipment, resulting in low production, high maintenance costs and lack of product uniformity.

Unrealistic depreciation charges can make profits look bigger. Then when equipment must be replaced the company finds it is no longer competitive. Recognize the changing value of the dollar and be realistic about costs and profits. Set your prices accordingly and plan the resources necessary for eventual replacement of equipment. You may find it is already far beyond the time when obsolete equipment should be replaced.

2. *Have you personally inspected the condition of your plant and equipment?* Touring your plant facilities and observing the processes and material flow may reveal to you an improper balance of equipment. Nothing beats a personal tour to uncover obvious equipment deficiencies. Remember, the production of a plant can only be as great as the volume of the slowest department. Carry a pad and pencil to make notes. Ask the foremen the types of problems they have been experiencing with your present facilities. Don't expect one visit to show up everything, but it should alert you to a host of opportunity areas for cost improvement.

3. *Do you own your plant and equipment outright?* Leasing equipment may have advantages over buying. Each time you need new or additional facilities evaluate leasing as a possible alternative to investing your own capital funds. With a minimum investment you may be able to get the equipment that is right for your department rather than to compromise on something which costs less, but doesn't really do the job as effectively. Therefore, look at all the cost aspects of each project, including its financing, and you may improve the overall cost picture by leasing rather than buying.

4. *Do you re-evaluate new plant and equipment projects after installation?* Unless you follow through to determine that anticipated cost savings are actually being realized, you may not be getting the full impact of improvement from the new costly machines. Although equipment is changed, surrounding procedures often fail to keep up. Of what use is a high speed machine if the production control department continues to schedule the shop at the old machine production rate. Review each capital project after it is in operation and if anticipated results are not achieved, find out why. Even if you are unable to improve that situation, you will obtain valuable information to assist your evaluation of the next project which is proposed.

Summary

The example questions above provide a framework of ideas to stimulate your review and development of possible cost improvement opportunities, which may be hidden in your working capital and fixed asset investment. Don't limit your review to the questions provided here. Every business or operation is somewhat different. Jot down investment areas which are peculiar to your business and explore the various ways each of them gives rise to costs in your organization. Then develop ideas to exploit the opportunities you have identified.

7 EVALUATING PRODUCT COSTS

The largest cost item on the profit and loss statement is usually product cost, which is composed of three elements: material, direct labor, and manufacturing overhead. These three elements vary in their proportions from company to company depending upon the type of business.

A distributor would have high material content since most of its products would simply be purchased for resale. Direct labor and overhead would probably consist of only warehouse and delivery costs. A manufacturing company could have a high proportion of each element depending on what it made and the extent to which it processed purchased material before it was converted to the finished product. For example, a company which assembles subcomponents into a finished product would have a high material content, since much of the product value is purchased. Such a company should give primary attention to its material costs but it is not unusual to find major attention given to controlling direct labor, which represents only a small percentage of its total product cost. Other manufacturing companies, even those which start with primary raw materials, may be so highly mechanized that overhead represents the largest percentage of their product costs.

Your chances of realizing substantial cost improvement will be greater if you first start with your company's major cost element in product costs. Don't forget that opportunities exist in all three of the cost elements, however, and none should be overlooked in a total cost management program.

Standard Cost Systems

Many companies use a standard cost system to control and account for product costs. A discussion of evaluating material, labor and overhead costs would not be complete without looking at standard cost systems from the manager's viewpoint.

Where a variety of products are produced on common equipment, from similar materials, with a common labor force, standard costs can be very useful in controlling and measuring the operations. If the standards are set properly, the overall variances between "standard" and "actual" costs will indicate either volume fluctuations or some deviation from the standard operation. Generally, it is an accounting function to analyze the period variations to ascertain that all costs were properly accounted for and that the variances are normal and explainable.

If you are a manufacturing manager, you should not only understand each variance and why the actual was different from standard but also realize that these cost variances may point out basic cost problems which need management attention. A thorough review of the basic causes for these cost variances may lead to many cost reduction opportunities. Here are some examples of what a detail study of variances can show:

Material Variances

Excessive costs because of material substitutes.

Poor discretion in utilizing material content to maximum advantage.

Material price increases which have not been reflected in the standard.

Labor Variances

Improper utilization of labor classifications.

Inadequate or excessive manning of machines.

Failure to run automatic machinery at maximum speeds.

Informal changes in production methods which have lowered production.

Labor rate increases which have not been reflected in the standard.

Overhead Variances

Excessive indirect labor costs due to improper scheduling or manpower control.

Overhead rates which do not include all the indirect departments.

Excessive maintenance costs and related idle time.

Excessive spending in other overhead costs.

A review of standard cost variances can also show that the standards themselves are incorrect or in need of revision. Standards may have been calculated incorrectly because the basic data was misinterpreted. Outdated bills of material can result in incorrect material standards, changes in labor methods can result in incorrect labor standards, and overhead changes can significantly affect overhead rates.

Most companies which use standard costs have industrial engineering and accounting departments who have the responsibility of keeping the detail standards up-to-date and correct. The individual manufacturing manager, however, should understand *how* the standards are constructed and applied in order to assure himself, (a) that all the direct product costs which should be included are; and, (b) what effect any changes he makes in his operation will have on the standard costs. In addition he should obtain answers to the following questions in order to pinpoint potential cost improvement opportunities.

1. *Are there too many different standards?* Excessive cost details may be maintained for similar items. Like products with different finishes or other minor variations can

be controlled by common standard costs. By keeping the number of different standards to a minimum substantial clerical savings in reporting labor time and production information can be obtained.

2. *How detailed are the standard cost breakdowns?* Component costs may be too detailed. Common inexpensive items such as washers, nuts, bolts, screws, etc., can often be handled as overhead. On the other hand there may not be enough breakdown of costs. The result then is that insufficient data will be available for evaluating costs.

Standard cost breakdowns should be adequate to give needed accuracy. They should not be so complex as to make them difficult to review and revise when needed.

3. *How closely were material costs reviewed before the standards were set?* When checking material prices for setting standards, investigate the differences. It may lead to disclosure that purchases are being made from high cost vendors. Standard costs can hide excessive costs if they are not reviewed objectively by someone independent of the purchasing department.

4. *Are the standards based on expected performance levels?* Standard costs often reflect only past performance experience. Small variances are satisfactory only if the standards exclude inefficient working conditions, methods, materials or machines. When these factors are buried, excessive costs cannot be pinpointed.

5. *Are the overhead standards based on practical capacity levels?* If the sales department is placing emphasis upon the sale of products based upon profit margins, it is extremely important to determine that proper overhead rates are set in those departments having mixed operations. As a convenience to the manufacturing operation, a product which requires the use of only one low overhead machine will often be manufactured in a department having other high cost pieces of equipment with their related maintenance costs, etc. If the full overhead rate for such a

department is applied to the simple product, an obvious distortion to that product's cost will result. Charged with the excessive overhead cost of the total department, it would no doubt appear to be a low margin item, when actually it could be highly profitable were costs assigned properly. Such cost distortions can even lead to a good product's elimination because of inaccurate cost information.

6. *Are the overhead rates too low?* If overhead rates are set too low there is the danger that prices will not include adequate provision for unabsorbed overhead. Overhead under-absorption may also not be spread equitably among all product lines when overall profit results are reviewed. Overhead rates should include all the costs which are properly assignable to the product. Failure to include all related product costs in standards which are used for establishment of prices can result in under pricing and reduction of potential revenues.

7. *Are the reasons for indirect labor known?* When direct laborers are idle because of machine breakdown, lack of material or other such reasons, do they charge their time to indirect labor accounts which indicate the reason why the cost was incurred?

Reporting idle time rather than applying an overall efficiency factor gives a more accurate cost. Failure to report idle time tends to bury cost in the variance account where it cannot be identified or controlled.

These are examples of the type of questions a manufacturing manager should ask about his standard cost system. Develop your own questions to enable you to evaluate the standard cost system used in your operations.

Now, let us review the three cost elements—material, direct labor, and manufacturing overhead—in more detail and explore specific ways to uncover possible cost improvements in the Product Cost area.

Material

Material is probably the most difficult cost element to tackle. Many managers feel that this cost is out of their control. How many times have you heard managers cite inflation and other beyond-their-control reasons for increases in their material costs? There are companies who do not really know how much material they have used until they take a physical inventory, which is both time-consuming and expensive. Because of the expense many companies take inventory only once a year. Then it is too late to start thinking about managing the cost of materials.

Despite the problems in managing material costs, it is by no means impossible. A small number of items usually make up the bulk of the cost and by concentrating management efforts on these a company can focus its attention where the greatest cost improvement opportunities exist. Too much effort can be spent on numerous small value items. The ABC Method discussed in connection with inventories in the last chapter can also be applied to cost management efforts in purchasing, production scheduling, scrap control, warehousing and other material cost areas.

For example, to identify cost improvement opportunities in purchased components, analyze the end products for which they are used. First, establish a list of every purchased item used in the end products. Second, determine the unit cost of each purchased item. This should be the current cost of the item in the quantity lots you normally order. Next, multiply the quantity of each item used per end product by the unit cost, to determine the total cost of that item in each product. Be sure to add like items together if they are used in different products on an interchangeable basis. Then re-sort the list of all the purchased items in descending order by total dollars of cost. Thus the highest total dollar cost component will be at the top of your list for investigation and analysis.

Now you have an ABC listing of purchased components. Once you have this ABC listing you will probably be surprised to find that 75% to 85% of the total purchased cost in your products is contained in the first 5% to 10% of the items rather than the whole list.

For emphasis, examine it another way. A screw costing one cent and used 1,000 times represents a cost of $10. A frame component costing $5 and used only twice in the product represents $10. A 10% cost improvement in the price of the frame components results in the same cost improvement as a 10% reduction in the cost of the screws. Getting a 10% reduction in the cost of the screws may not be difficult by using quantity buying techniques.

This example is oversimplified but it shows that it is not always obvious where the cost improvement opportunities hide. Without knowing the usage and extended cost, would you have explored the possibility of reducing cost of the product by looking at the cost of penny screws?

A Team Approach for Managing Material Costs

The management of material costs requires joint programs by several departments in the average business.

1. A constant program to lower the purchase cost of materials by the Purchasing Department.

2. A continuing program to improve the design of the product in order to use less material or substitute less expensive materials by the Engineering Department; and

3. A program of continuing surveillance by the Sales Department so that prices are raised promptly when unavoidable price increases in material occur, thereby passing on the added cost to the customer.

This need for a team effort to attack material costs on all three fronts is perhaps why businesses consider material cost improvements the most difficult to achieve. However, material costs often represent such a substantial portion of total costs that only a small percentage improvement can make a major contribution to overall profits.

Using the ABC approach to identify the major opportunity areas, together with the Team Approach indicated to concentrate management attention, can result in dynamic improvements in material costs.

Direct Labor

The competitive conditions of today's industry have caused a tremendous increase in the use of automated equipment. As a result, direct labor cost has become a smaller percentage of total costs. In many companies, however, direct labor still represents a major cost which must be carefully managed.

Some companies have elaborate monitoring systems which use labor standards and various forms of productivity reports to provide enormous amounts of data on labor cost. Although these systems provide information on actual performance, they often fail to keep labor costs at minimum levels.

Earlier in this chapter we discussed standard cost systems on an overall basis. These standard cost systems seem to fail for measuring labor costs in four ways:

1. The systems provide only *data*. Managers don't always use the data or they use it simply as a club to make laborers work harder, rather than to use it to identify areas where opportunities exist for implementing cost improvement ideas.

2. Often actual times recorded by these systems are inaccurate. Either the employee, himself, or his foreman record the actual time for input into the system. Human nature tends to favor the recording of actual time in a manner which will minimize variances from standard. Operations having standards which are known to be "fat" will be charged more than actual time required; whereas, operations having standards which are considered "tight" will not be charged with the full time actually required. This makes both the worker and his foreman look better in the eyes of higher management, but does not reveal the problem area.

3. The standards, themselves, are often inaccurate. Changes in methods of manufacture, introduction of automated equipment and changes in production flow, present the costly task of continually keeping standards up-to-date. This is often not done on a timely basis, thus negating the effectiveness of measurement in the affected areas.

4. It is not always possible to accurately standardize labor operations for measurement of every operation.

Before tackling the problem of managing direct labor costs, you must first evaluate the standard cost system itself to determine its effectiveness at your company.

A Simplified Approach
for Measuring Direct Labor Productivity

Many companies do not have a formal standard labor cost system; or, after reading the problems indicated above, you may decide that the one you have is not as effective as you had previously thought. It may be more useful to look at direct labor on an overall basis rather than studying detail operations.

If you have a standard cost system, add up the standard hours from all operations needed to produce a given product, or sub-assembly. The inaccuracies in the individual operation standards will average out when you look at the total labor content in a product.

If you don't have a standard cost system, make some overall estimates as to what the labor content should be based on industry averages or your past experiences with similar products.

Next, take a larger period of time. Instead of looking at the units produced in an hour, take the time period of a week. Labor hours for a week may be gleaned from payroll records rather than individual operation time cards. The actual time expended to produce the product will be more accurate if taken from the labor hours paid for, rather than what was reported against standards.

For example: Suppose in this week 6,000 units were completed. Assume your total labor based on totalling the standard operations or your estimates, should be one-half hour per unit. Thus, the total earned hours were 3,000 (6,000 times 1/2 hour). The actual number of hours paid for, according to payroll records, was 4,800 to complete those 6,000 units. Thus, the percentage of efficiency was 62.5% (3,000 earned hours divided by 4,800 actual hours).

By using this overall method you include the hours expended by the direct labor force on such tasks as material handling, rework and lost time because of machine breakdowns, which would normally be classified as indirect labor. Foremen often fail to provide for this indirect labor element performed by the direct labor force when they prepare their estimates of indirect labor.

Comparing this overall efficiency percentage over a period of weeks can be as effective in measuring direct labor performance as the most sophisticated cost systems, and a lot less costly. Also, since this labor cost information is developed by product, a list of products in descending order of their total labor content can be made to utilize the ABC approach for evaluating labor costs. As with purchased material, it would not be surprising to find 80% of the labor cost in the first 20% of the list. It is a lot easier to concentrate your efforts on those 15 or 20 products or sub-assemblies which constitute the major labor cost rather than on the entire product line.

Let Labor Work Smarter Not Harder.

Looking at products on a labor content basis is easier than looking at direct labor in total. Each product or sub-assembly can now be evaluated with the goal of reducing its total labor content. As you evaluate each, ask questions similar to the following:

1. Can the product be subcontracted or purchased outright at less cost?
2. Would new equipment reduce labor required through greater automation?

3. Is too much time being expended on indirect operations rather than direct production efforts?
4. Can some of the operations be combined or eliminated?
5. Was this much labor content considered in setting the selling price of the product?
6. Can the product be redesigned to eliminate labor costs?
7. Can production methods be changed to eliminate labor effort and time?
8. Would better scheduling eliminate bottlenecks which are causing lost time?
9. Are direct labor hours being wasted, while workers wait for material, cranes, or machine paced operations?
10. Is poor supervision resulting in excessive break periods, start-up times, and shift change lags?

Each of the above examples is aimed at reducing labor effort by producing the product more effectively, not by making individual laborers work harder. Aim your attack on labor costs with the objective of doing less to produce more, rather than trying to work harder. It's easier and far more effective.

Manufacturing Overhead

The major overhead element in product costs is generally that associated with the manufacturing operations. There may also be warehousing and delivery costs in overhead charges.

We usually think of overhead as those costs which can not be directly identified and charged directly to the individual products as easily as are material and direct labor costs. Supervision and clerical salaries, indirect labor such as material handlers and maintenance men, indirect materials and supplies, small tools, purchased services such as utilities and guard services, payroll related taxes and insurance, and fixed charges such as depreciation, real estate taxes, and fire insurance are a few examples. Although all are necessary costs which must be incurred, they cannot be directly associated with individual products. Thus, they are often controlled through the use of budgets which are based on past experience or expected volumes.

Since manufacturing overhead is a "catchall" for everything that isn't readily classified as material or direct labor, it often becomes inflated with unnecessary costs. Often, manufacturing overheads are not questioned as rigorously as operating expense overhead; such as, general and administrative, or selling expenses, since they are justified on a blanket basis as a percentage of direct labor dollars. Sometimes manufacturing overheads are substantially larger than operating expenses of the general and administrative or selling category, yet they are evaluated by higher management simply by comparing this year's overhead rate (percentage of overhead to direct labor) to the overhead rate in past periods.

Although some manufacturing overhead costs may vary directly with the labor force, many can and should be evaluated individually and justified based on actual need.

When volumes go down and large amounts of unabsorbed overhead takes their toll on profits, plant managers are quick to point out the fixed nature of their costs. When volumes go up overhead costs often rise as fast or faster than other costs.

Actually, all costs are variable with production over the long run and most are variable with and should respond to fluctuations of short duration. With that in mind, they should be understood and evaluated in the same manner as any other costs, using the six-step cost management approach.

First, look at the overall operations and then the more detail functions by utilizing the technique of asking questions which identify cost improvement opportunity areas.

The example questions given here are for the purpose of stimulating your thoughts about your own operations in all cost areas. Later we will discuss questions about specific overhead costs.

General Questions to Ask About Manufacturing Operations

1. *Does manufacturing know its individual product costs?* This question may sound very academic but the amazing fact is few manufacturing managers know and understand the detailed cost of the products they produce. Remember that reference here to management means all levels, including shop floor foremen.

Sometimes detail cost information is kept secret, presumably for competitive reasons. The wisdom of this secrecy is doubtful. The front line foreman initiates most of the action which generates cost in a manufacturing operation. He may not actually hire the direct and indirect worker, but he generally assigns the tasks that utilize and expend this company resource. The foreman usually does not select or buy the material used in the products, but it is he that directs its consumption. Also, it is the shop floor foreman who initiates and directs the operations which result in the bulk of the overhead incurred in the manufacturing operations.

By withholding detail cost information from these key management members, in effect you relieve him from his natural responsibility to control these costs. After all, if he has no knowledge of them, never has the opportunity to compare actual cost performance against what is considered normal or standard, then he cannot possibly be expected to improve cost performance by developing improved operations.

So it is with the first level manager in production control, inspection, quality control, assembly, shipping, maintenance, etc., each must know the cost of his operations before you can expect him to care about eliminating or preventing unnecessary costs.

Look at your manufacturing operations. Just who does get actual cost information? Are they held responsible for the costs that their operations incur? Or, are costs a big dark secret known only to a select few at the very top of the pyramid?

2. *Have you considered moving, adding or discontinuing plant locations?* Sources of material or labor, accessibility to supply, or changes in method of transporting material and products are in constant change.

Do your financial statements show profit figures by location? When was the last time you reviewed the location of your major suppliers and customers?

Most companies evaluate these factors when they establish new operations, but many fail to review existing operations periodically. The cost savings in freight alone can often justify the relocation of operations. Don't let that "we've always been here" attitude stop you from at least considering this suggestion. Evaluate the location of existing plants and other operations as thoroughly as you would the setting up of a new operation or expansion. Many times a change in location can open new opportunities that were not previously considered.

3. *How often are manufacturing methods reviewed?* How often have you heard a manufacturing manager brag that he's been able to keep some old piece of machinery producing at almost the same rate it did when it was first installed twenty years ago? He feels this feat has been a real cost saving.

If he happens to be manufacturing buggy whips, he may be right; but, many industries have seen a more rapid rate of technological change. If a manufacturing operation is performing its functions today the same way it did four or five years ago, it is probably losing ground to its more advanced competitors. New products replace old ones. New equipment developments enable greater production efficiencies. A company can fail to take advantage of these advancements unless manufacturing methods and products are reviewed periodically.

Another reason that methods should be reviewed periodically is to correct "informal" changes. Manual production methods are seldom documented in instruction manuals. With employee turnover in both supervisory and labor, informal changes creep in.

A sawing operation is a good example. The original standard method may have called for cutting six pieces at one time. A periodic method review, which compares actual methods to those used to develop the standard costs, may show that the method currently being used is to cut one piece at a time. There may have been a good reason when the change was made. Maybe a special order with different materials required the change, but somehow the original method was not reinstated and used after the special order was completed.

This example shows only one small change that may not have much effect on the overall efficiency of the operation; but, multiply it by the hundreds of operations in most shops and you can quickly see that informal method changes can have a dynamic effect on production capabilities.

If you haven't had a thorough review of manufacturing methods in your shop in the last year, you probably have a significant cost improvement opportunity which should be explored.

4. *Who schedules production?* I don't mean who is *supposed* to schedule production, I mean who actually decides what is going to be produced today. Is it really the production control department? Or, is it the sales department who has gotten special changes from the official production schedule in order to expedite a favored customer's order? Or, is it the line foreman basing his schedule on the material he happens to have on hand.

Plant management must schedule and control production, otherwise they cannot be held responsible for production results.

Don't take for granted that because you have formal production schedules it is actually happening that way. Find out what is actually happening, you may be surprised.

5. *Are production schedules based on long and short range sales forecacts?* Sales forecasting is not getting the attention it deserves. Too often sales forecasts represent

only optimistic hopes of the sales department without adequate review and evaluation by the other functions, such as manufacturing, who rely on them.

Nothing is more devastating to a manufacturing manager's plans than to have sales orders flow into his plant at levels substantially below the sales forecast, upon which his plans were based. Even more disastrous as the year continues is the reluctance of that sales department to revise their estimates so that manufacturing can cut back their operations to coincide with current order demand.

Many of us have experienced the sales manager who constantly states, "this period was a little slow, but we expect to make it up next period."

Coordination between sales and manufacturing is essential to plan production in a manner which can achieve optimum cost effectiveness. How accurate are your sales forecasts? Especially the short-range ones which enable the manufacturing manager to plan his operations next week and next month.

Where schedules are based on accurate sales input, are the schedules followed or are they modified so much that manufacturing ignores them? Production schedules that change from day-to-day serve little or no purpose. Labor and material must be scheduled further in advance to assure availability. The reaction time for most overhead costs is even longer.

6. *Are schedule problems influenced by internal or external events?* Absenteeism, inadequate production facilities, poor material control, lack of qualified personnel, etc., represent internal problems which manufacturing management can handle. Absenteeism may require stricter discipline; additional capital investment can upgrade production facilities; improved procedures can provide better balanced inventories; and programs which improve morale levels may attract more qualified workers; all actions which manufacturing management can take to correct their schedule problems.

External influences such as vendors who constantly fail

to meet delivery requirements, customers who constantly demand special delivery times, and critical shortages of key materials usually require action by functions outside of manufacturing. Manufacturing management must get together with the representatives of these other functions to correct the problem.

Perhaps the purchasing department can find a more reliable supplier, even if it means spending extra money; the sales department may have to make firmer policies regarding order delivery promises; or top management may have to approach government agencies to secure critical materials. Identify what is causing your production schedule problems, then tackle each one as a separate problem in the manner needed because of its unique characteristics.

7. *How effectively is the major equipment in the shop utilized?* Some plants allow major pieces of production equipment to stand idle when backlogs are available to keep them busy. This is even more critical if lack of machine capacity is holding up other operations.

Consider having a short overlapping of shifts. An overlap of only five minutes can result in a major productivity gain. Machines that are usually shut down before the end of the shift can be kept in operation. You would be amazed at the amount of production time that is wasted between shifts. Employees may shut down machines several minutes before the end of the shift in order to have time for cleanup before quitting time. Second shift employees seldom start up the equipment immediately since they often wait for instructions from their foremen. Unless closely supervised, workers may tend to expand the brief shut down for half an hour or more.

Companies that operate two shifts per day can easily arrange for the required overlap of shifts. If a plant is operating three shifts, overlapping will require paying some overtime, but it is a small price compared to the substantial gain in equipment utilization.

One plant in particular used a computer to monitor critical pieces of equipment. The computer simply recorded whether a machine was in operation or not. This computer poll was made every five minutes by attaching thermocouples to the equipment which were connected to the computer by telephone lines. The mass of "On/Off" answers was then summarized and plotted on a graph for management review. Initial surveys made this way showed as much as an hour of idle time between shifts on equipment that had months of backlog waiting for machine time. By arranging for overlapping shifts and staggered break times, they were able to keep the equipment running an extra four hours per day. Since the five pieces of equipment monitored in this trial review cost in excess of one million dollars each, you can realize the substantial productivity gain from utilizing each one an additional four hours per day. The twenty hours of additional capacity per day was equivalent to having purchased a sixth machine—but without additional investment and without hiring a sixth crew to operate it.

8. *Does the manufacturing area have too many or too few machines?* Most companies experience volume changes in their various product lines. Some products become obsolete, some are eliminated; at the same time new products are developed to replace the lost volume. This change in products often requires new and different types of equipment.

Periodically, a study should be made to determine if proper equipment is available to produce the company's current product lines, also if there are too few or too many machines for the current forecasted production levels. New product lines often grow rapidly after their initial introduction and cause a scarcity of machines to produce them. Unless older equipment is adaptable to production of the new products, the older machinery becomes idle as the older product lines decrease in volume.

Although the manufacturing plant has a substantial investment in total equipment, an equipment study may show it actually has too few machines capable of producing its current products effectively. If this is so, then it must ask several other questions. If there are not enough machines, should it buy or rent more? What is the long-range potential for its new products? Should new or used equipment be bought? How fast will the new equipment depreciate?

The study will also raise questions about the older equipment that is becoming idle. Should the company sell this excess or should they seek more business? What is the long-range outlook for the older product lines? If additional volumes for the older products are possible, will additional promotional costs to gain that volume level offset the potential additional margins?

Equipment studies should be conducted at least annually. Used machines which are standing idle may be sold for more than present book value. By reinvesting the funds from the sale of old equipment in machines which produce the new product lines more efficiently, substantial profit improvement can be possible.

Because of long lead times required to install newer equipment, a company's profit potential can be delayed several months, perhaps even cause it to lose its chance to get ahead of competitors when a new product is introduced. A continuing program of evaluating equipment utilization and needs can prevent this loss of profits.

9. *Are set up times studied to determine optimum production runs?* Continued management pressure to keep inventory investment low can cause manufacturing supervision to forget the impact of set up time on their operating costs. In lowering the size of production run volumes to meet inventory investment objectives, they may find that their production costs have soared.

By studying set up times and related costs for each machine or operation and comparing these costs per unit with inventory carrying costs for individual products, it is possible to determine an optimum production run size. Similar products that require the same set up procedures can often be scheduled so that separate set ups can be eliminated. A forward look at incoming orders may make possible the grouping of orders requiring like components thus eliminating unnecessary set up time, especially when many small orders may be causing the same set up operations two or three times in the same day or week.

Here is another area where production line workers can give valuable suggestions. A machine operator who must make the same set up several times a week will think that "management doesn't know what they are doing," or more important, cause him to have a careless attitude since nobody else seems to care about him and his job.

Don't rely on the Production Control Department's assurance that they have obtained the optimum level for production runs. Ask the machine operator himself. His answers may surprise you.

10. *Have you compared the production schedule to actual output?* Some plants require this to be done on a regular basis. However, is an attempt made to find reasons for differences and subsequent follow-up to eliminate any problems uncovered?

When production does not meet expected schedules, often the problem is unrealistic schedule expectations. Even the best schedules are not always met, but realistic schedules should result in "ahead of schedule" conditions at times. If your expected production level is never attained, then it is probably based on invalid assumptions about machine speeds, set up times, material availability, etc.

Sales forecasts, cost calculations, and other information which affect management decisions are based on the production schedule. Management assumes that what is scheduled will be produced. Constant failure to meet production schedules causes incorrect management decisions, late customer deliveries, and even loss of customers when relied upon promises are not kept.

Comparing actual production to expected schedule levels with proper follow-up can prevent these problems and often lead to cost improvements.

11. *Have you reviewed the flow of work through the manufacturing areas?* Often the only reason that one opera-

tion is performed before another is because it has always been done that way. New products are squeezed in between other lines until there is little semblance of order on the production floor. Management sometimes uses the excuse of increased one time costs to refrain from making necessary rearrangements of equipment for more efficient work flow. Avoiding rearrangement costs may be valid when only limited new product operations are added. However, when there has been a rapid change in customer requirements, the cumulative effect over a period of time can be substantial.

Sometimes a study of the various operations will show that rearrangement is not necessary. Simply performing the operations in a different order will improve production volume. For example, the following:

Windows were completely assembled in the plant and then shipped to distribution centers for ultimate sale to builders. However, the builders wanted the *frames* delivered for installation when the cement block was being put in place, the *window panels* delivered for installation after the rough interior work was done, and the *screens* delivered at the final completion of the house. To comply with the builder's delivery instructions, it was necessary to disassemble the frames, panels and screens for separate delivery by the distribution branch.

Substantial savings were realized when the plant started to ship unassembled frames, panels, and screens. By scheduling the three components for shipment to the branch on a timetable which approximated subsequent delivery to the builders, inventories could also be kept at a lower level.

Take a look at your shop work flow and the order in which the various operations take place. You may find not only cost savings, but ways to lower inventory investment or to reduce the production span by paralleling operations.

12. *How effective are your material handling techniques and equipment?* Often, a substantial amount of the indirect labor and related costs in a plant is expended on material

handling. No matter how streamlined a plant's operations may be, sooner or later the products require movement to another department.

There have been many improved types of handling equipment developed and put on the market. If your plant hasn't made a study of this cost area recently, then it could be ripe for cost improvement.

The study should evaluate the time spent, necessity, method and cost of the movements being made throughout the work flow. Start at the point raw materials are first received and follow the product flow until it leaves the plant as a finished product.

Time spent in moving goods from one section of the plant to another not only costs money but slows down the productive cycle. Unnecessary moves, particularly moves back and forth between departments when a number of operations could be accomplished before transfer of the material, builds in excessive handling costs. Actually drawing a diagram of the product movement will point out the more obvious waste of this kind.

Methods used are equally important. Movement of material can be accomplished by workers, forklift trucks, cranes, conveyor belts, etc. Storage between moves may be in bins, on pallets, shelves, or racks, or simply in stacks or cartons. The trick is to find the optimum method which requires the minimum human effort, the least time, and also minimizes cost. The company must always consider workers' safety and exposure of the various products to potential damage.

Chart the flow of materials and indicate the method used for each move. Then redraft a material flow whereby as much work as possible is done at each work area at one time, followed by movement of material only when necessary by the most economical method. Economics must include loading and unloading costs as well as the actual movement costs.

Improving material handling may mean rearrangement of whole departments in order to get an optimum flow.

Remember the shortest distance between receipt of material and shipment of the finished product is usually a straight line.

13. *Is each manufacturing department or operation necessary?* Sometimes manufacturing operations can be combined, inspection points eliminated, even whole departments consolidated. That doesn't mean their function was unnecessary but supervisory costs can be reduced even when the same tasks are still being performed.

Be careful when you combine responsibilities that *needed* quality standards are not relaxed in the rush to reduce costs. Also, remember that the reduction of supervision can result in higher labor costs. Obtaining the right balance between supervision, quality and labor efficiency can be tricky; but, excessive supervision builds in unnecessary costs.

Look for functions which are performed by one department which could just as easily be completed in another department, or for similar operations being performed in several departments. For example:

A company had several product lines, each of which was produced totally in separate work centers. Each work center had cutting and punching operations. Because of fluctuations in sales volume, the activities in each work center had extreme volume fluctuations. By combining the cutting and punching operations under one foreman a more level load was achieved. This operation then supplied component parts to each of the assembly areas. Assembly crews were then retrained to be proficient on more than one of the product assembly lines. By shifting assembly crews between product lines based on volume requirements, substantial labor savings were realized.

Specific Questions About Manufacturing Operations

The foregoing questions are of a broad general nature which not only identify overhead savings opportunities, but also point out savings in material and direct labor areas. To explore the opportunities in the overhead areas, it is necessary to look at specific cost areas on a more detail basis. For example, here are some questions you could ask about your shipping costs.

1. *When was the last time you personally inspected the shipping department?* Nothing beats this for a simple way to find out obvious things being done which are giving rise to unnecessary costs. Carry a pad and pencil to jot down notes. Don't expect one visit to show up everything. Keep on making periodic visits throughout the year. It's surprising how many cost savings can be detected by taking an objective, on-the-spot look at operations.

2. *Do you invite competitive bids on transport services?* Shipping foremen or traffic managers are often so hard pressed to ship on schedule that they don't take the time to analyze competing services closely and to select the most cost effective. Although inviting bids and comparing transport companies is a basic cost control rule, it isn't always done. Companies often fall into the rut of using the same transport service year after year. A continuing review in this area will usually yield savings. At least you will satisfy yourself that the decisions being made are the right ones.

3. *Do your trucking companies have "incentive rates"?* Trucking companies lose money handling small shipments. Many offer shippers a discount for combining several small orders into single large loads. If you are willing to delay a few small orders until you are able to make up a large load, it can result in substantial savings.

4. *Do you use Air Freight as an alternative to other forms of transportation?* Air Freight rates have changed considerably over the years. Depending on your products' value and density, delivery requirements and other factors, air freight can be very competitive with other forms of transportation. Be sure to consider your present warehousing concepts and costs of carrying inventories, if this is a factor in getting faster deliveries to customers. Often the customer is willing to pay a higher freight cost if it helps

to keep warehousing costs down. The high cost of borrowed capital can change his way of looking at things too. Centralizing warehouses and using air freight to speed deliveries can be a cost saver for both you and your customer.

5. *Have you reviewed your shipping schedules in the last few months?* Shipping schedules are often set up at the request of the sales department to satisfy special customer demands. The cost of any special shipping schedule which causes less than truckload rates is often out of proportion to the business special customers are actually giving you. Customer requirements change but such information doesn't always get communicated to the shipping department. Start by asking which customers have special arrangements. Then talk to the sales department and find out why.

6. *Does your shipper have special rates for off-peak shipments?* Transport companies also have their busy times followed by relatively quiet periods. Sometimes you can cut your costs by negotiating an incentive for shipping during the slow periods.

7. *Do you review your shipment packing to assure getting the best rate classification?* A shipment could be classified at a higher rate simply because it hasn't been packed in the manner required for a lower rating. The cost of packing must also be considered in this evaluation.

For example, when two or more products are packed together, the highest rated item normally determines the entire charge on a less-than-carload shipment. Also, insurance charges on a shipment can be increased by including one high value item.

8. *How accurate are your bill of lading descriptions?* Are you describing your product on the bill of lading so that it qualifies for the lowest rate classification? Review your product descriptions to make sure you are getting the lowest freight rate. Sometimes the inclusion of a single component in a finished product will change its classification to a higher rate.

9. *Do your truck drivers notify customers of their estimated arrival time?* A lot of time can be wasted by your drivers waiting for unloading space and for help at the customer's warehouse. By having your drivers call each customer about 30 minutes in advance of his arrival, you can often eliminate much of his waiting time.

10. *Do you reuse your supplier's shipping containers?* With the cost of packing material increasing dramatically these days, it pays to use every available means to keep the cost down. Savings can be especially good if your supplier's containers readily lend themselves to reuse by simply affixing new labels and shipping instructions.

11. *Is all your packaging really necessary?* A periodic review of the way you package your product can often lead to savings. With the many new packaging materials on the market, the field has become very competitive. Large packaging manufacturers employ trained representatives who are eager to give their advice on how to cut packaging costs, especially if you agree to use their packaging products.

12. *How do you handle freight charges on small orders?* Many companies discourage small orders by establishing a minimum charge, or by refusing to handle any order below a certain amount. If you are already paying the freight on shipments of your products, consider requiring the customer to pay the freight only on orders under a specified amount. This has the effect of offering your customers an incentive to order in large quantities, and at the same time of eliminating shipping charges on the small orders.

Looking At Specific Overhead Costs
The example questions on the previous pages have been aimed at evaluating the general and specific manufacturing operations. It is also necessary to look at specific overhead cost items, some of which may be common to all areas of the plant.

Salaries

Supervision and clerical salaries in a manufacturing plant represent a substantial portion of the overhead. Plant salaries can and should be evaluated by conducting a staffing review like the example given in Chapter 4. Such a review establishes what each salaried person is doing, which enables the manager to evaluate the need and importance of what is actually taking place.

Unfortunately, many companies take the position that a detail study of shop supervisory personnel is unnecessary. Everybody knows from experience the supervision required for the number of direct labor persons employed. The trouble with this attitude is that many supervisors in industry spend very little of their time supervising. A detail staffing review may point out some of the following:

1. The great percentage of their time is spent performing clerical tasks which could be more economically performed by a centralized clerk who can assist several foremen.

2. Many of their tasks require them to leave the plant area for which they are responsible. Have you often wondered who is giving direction to the laborers when the foreman is attending the variety of meetings which many managements require?

3. Substantial amounts of their time is spent trying to locate material which never seems to be *where* it should, *when* it should. Many companies now use lower paid floor expeditors to assist foremen with this problem.

4. Where standard costs are in use, many foremen spend unnecessary amounts of time trying to have as many operations as possible taken "off standard" or to "beat the system" in a variety of other ways.

5. When production drawings or instructions are vague, foremen spend too much time simply trying to figure out what is required. They may come up with answers which ultimately result in even greater problems.

In some staffing reviews it has been found that foremen

actually spent less than 25% of their time doing their formally assigned job; i.e., that of planning, assigning, directing and controlling the activities of the labor force.

Don't fail to conduct a staffing review of shop supervisory activities. Then use the data to get greater utilization of supervisors, as well as clerical personnel.

Indirect Labor

Indirect labor is most frequently the cost element that gets out of hand in a manufacturing operation thereby offering fertile opportunities for cost improvement. Indirect labor should be controlled as carefully as direct labor, indeed if not more so. Many companies spend enormous amounts of time and money attempting to measure and control the productivity of direct labor then do little, if anything, to measure and control indirect labor. Indirect labor in these companies can represent a dollar cost almost as large as the cost of direct labor.

For purposes of our discussion, let's divide *indirect* labor into three categories:

1. Permanently assigned or designated labor such as; material handlers, maintenance men, receiving and shipping personnel, etc.
2. Direct labor employees who temporarily perform indirect labor functions and as a result charge indirect labor overhead accounts.
3. Overtime premium costs of both direct and indirect labor which many companies classify as an indirect labor charge.

First, let's look at permanently assigned or designated indirect labor. The time of individuals in this category is usually a 100% charge to overhead. To reduce the cost of this overhead element requires eliminating or avoiding the need for the tasks they perform.

Start by observing in some detail just what all the individuals in this category are doing. Because you have always had eight material handlers in the warehouse is not a reason for continuing to have that many. Look at the crew sizes, the activity level, the equipment available, and how effectively they are supervised. Now ask yourself: What can be eliminated? What are we doing which can be avoided? How can we simplify this function? Do we really need this many people to do the job?

If you can eliminate the need or simplify the task, then the cost improvements become readily apparent.

Now, compare the cost of these service functions with outside costs of these services. For example: In-house guards can be replaced with outside guard services; Warehouse labor can sometimes be replaced by companies who run public warehousing operations; In-house maintenance by sub-contracted repairs; etc.

Next, examine the projects this indirect labor is working on. Are maintenance projects carefully controlled and approved before work is started? Are the costs of the project charged back to the department or function which requested it? Is there a continuing preventative maintenance program or is everything done on a crash basis? Try to identify projects which are initiated simply to keep crews busy during low volume periods. Just because workers are available doesn't mean they have to be used on unnecessary projects. These temporarily idle employees can often be used in another department which really needs an important project completed.

Take a close look at the material handling activities; these are an unrecognized major element of cost. Minimization of physical handling can often be accomplished through the use of mechanized conveyors, gravity chutes and continuous process lines, which means substantial cost savings. Arrange materials in proper order to facilitate pickup for order filling, an elementary but often overlooked time saver.

Sometimes by centralizing overall supervision of major indirect service activities, i.e., a shop superintendent over warehousing, material handling, maintenance, etc., you can get greater utilization of indirect labor.

After identifying and eliminating unnecessary projects and activities, transfer the excess labor to direct labor assignments in order to remove them from the indirect payroll. Keep in mind Parkinson's Law "Work expands to fill available time."

The next category of indirect labor are those costs charged by temporarily idle direct labor performing indirect tasks. Human nature, and foremen who want to improve their direct labor productivity report, can have a substantial impact on this category of cost. Review these costs to prevent improper charges to indirect labor. Be on the lookout for foremen who hoard labor by transferring productive workers to indirect labor to avoid layoffs. Make sure the accounting system is reporting this indirect labor accurately.

Indirect labor costs in this category should be minimal. If your review shows a substantial percentage of indirect labor resulting from direct labor personnel charging indirect labor accounts, then your direct labor force needs a review which in all probability will identify the need for a layoff.

The third category, that of overtime premium, should never be allowed to get very high before a review is made to determine what should be done. Excessive recurring overtime generally indicates an unbalanced operation, a breakdown in scheduling and production control activities, or improper loading of various departments.

Watch this indicator. If overtime rises, investigate the cause, especially if you have a low fixed asset investment.

Indirect Materials

Many companies, which do an excellent job of controlling direct materials, completely overlook indirect materials which are charged to manufacturing overhead rather than directly to the product. Perhaps this is because their quantities and costs are so much less than direct materials; but, machine repair parts, small tools, and other shop supplies can add up to a significant total cost.

Like most overhead expenses they are usually controlled by establishing budgets based on experience, or on a percentage of direct labor or on some other indicator of volume level. The mere establishment of a budget for these expense items is a strong force toward controlling unnecessary cost. The establishment of direct controls over indirect material costs is more effective, however.

For example, do you have secured areas with access limited to authorized personnel for machine repair parts and other operating supply inventories? Leaving these items open for use without physical control is sure to result in their misuse. One review of the cost of supplies at a plant revealed that there were enough flashlights being purchased to supply every employee with a new one every month. Work gloves were also being issued in abnormally high quantities. By requiring the damaged or worn out item to be turned in before a new one could be issued, the cost of these items dropped significantly.

Develop physical ways to control the issuance and use of supply items and you will have a much greater control than the best paperwork system.

Small tools are another example. When small tools are not subject to direct controls, overall tool costs frequently are out of line. Greater control over such expenditures can be made, by studying consumption to identify unusual trends, by establishing physical controls over issues, and by a more critical observation of repair and replacement requests.

Maintenance Costs

Both indirect labor and indirect material costs are often affected by the way maintenance costs are managed. Maintenance costs frequently become excessive because of problems in controlling such expense. Improvement in these costs can be achieved by establishing a maintenance work order system which requires accurate reporting of labor and material used for each project. Also, by reviewing the material records for usage of repair parts, often purchasing economics can be effected or reductions in maintenance inventories. Rapid accumulation of costs by accounting can be effective in alerting management to project overruns.

Some companies have experienced excellent results in reducing maintenance costs by maintaining trend records which indicate frequency of replacement, size of orders, and proper utilization of machines. Such data leads naturally to the establishment of standards to measure performance, standard maintenance procedures and preventive maintenance programs.

Excessive repair and maintenance expense may also reflect the need for an equipment analysis. Without a work order system to provide historical information by major pieces of equipment, this condition can remain hidden.

A work order system also provides total cost by project of in-house maintenance for comparison with other alternatives. Savings can sometimes be achieved by subcontracting machine overhauling, for example, rather than by using company maintenance.

Other Overhead Costs

I have discussed only a few specific overhead costs that apply to most operations. You must take the list of overhead costs from your particular operation and look at each one individually.

For example, at your next staff meeting review the list of the overhead expenses item by item and develop ideas and programs to decrease each one by some amount. An hour spent developing cost decreases will pay for the meeting several times over.

Discussing a sales increase program, though beneficial on a long-term basis, will not have the immediate impact on bottom line profits that the hour spent brainstorming cost improvements can accomplish.

There are two ways to increase profit, either by increasing sales volume or decreasing costs. If a company's sales generate a gross margin of 20% and operating expenses are 15%, leaving a profit before tax of 5%, an additional $1,000 of sales will generate only $50 more pretax profit. That same $50 increase could also be achieved by eliminating one telephone extension which costs approximately $5 per month or $60 annually.

The simple act of eliminating a single telephone extension is usually much easier and simpler to accomplish than adding the additional $1,000 sales volume.

Summary

In order to evaluate Product Costs you must first understand and evaluate each of its major elements—material, direct labor, and overhead. Although approached somewhat differently, each must answer satisfactorily the same question, "Is it necessary?"

Product Costs are related to volume but must also be thoroughly examined both from an operational, or functional view, and on a specific item-by-item basis.

By using the ABC approach which stratifies the major cost items at the top of your list, you can focus your attention on the major opportunities first. But, don't neglect small improvements which can add up to substantial amounts.

To disclose inefficiencies and ineffective operations you must ask many How, What, Where and Why type questions. You must question methods and procedures; probe into the basic requirements; question the necessity for present operations; and evaluate the effectiveness of methods presently being used. As you understand each operation or identify needed improvements, jot them down for future reference in developing your cost improvement ideas.

8 MANAGING COMMON OFFICE COSTS

The average business today can cut office costs 20% or more by applying more management attention to common office costs. Expense areas; such as telephones, postage, office supplies, and other general office costs, which are not the responsibility of any one manager, offer major opportunities for cost improvement. Such costs are incurred by every department but none represent any individual department's major cost elements. Department managers tend to concentrate their cost reduction efforts on costs which are considered more important to their particular operations. These "minor" department expenses, which often represent a substantial total cost for the company, are thus given little management attention.

Dynamic cost improvements can be generated by simply analyzing and evaluating these common office costs on an overall company basis. Start by making someone responsible for these common office costs. Then use the Six-Step Cost Management Approach to eliminate the waste in these common expense areas.

Telephones

Telephones, once considered a luxury, are today a definite necessity in virtually every home and business. In many offices they have become a form of status symbol. A new employee is not considered a part of the organization until his phone has been installed. The junior manager hasn't really arrived until his phone has several buttons on it and an intercom with his secretary. Executives often feel that speaker phones, card dialing phones and private lines in their office are necessary. If you don't believe that phone equipment has become a status symbol in your company, try asking one of your subordinates to remove some of the frills from his phone equipment. Be ready for his many reasons why he needs more, not fewer, attachments.

In addition to unnecessary equipment most offices incur unnecessary long distance costs. It is not unusual to cut long distance costs by 50% or more while improving the effectiveness of the operation.

But how does the average manager attack the problem of eliminating unnecessary telephone costs? Start by analyzing all telephone bills for the past three months. Bills differ from state to state and/or from different telephone companies, but they all show basic equipment charges, long distance calls, and in some locations message unit charges.

The Basic Equipment 'Charge

Billed one month in advance this amount represents the monthly charge for renting your equipment from the telephone company. Even in a small office it may be a thousand dollars or more.

Many companies pay this without question. The telephone bill gives no detail information on the actual equipment in use. To analyze this monthly cost you must obtain an itemized statement from your telephone company business office. Usually it is a computer form which shows the cost of each instrument and all its supplementary equipment.

Your first step is to take a complete inventory of equipment which is actually in use and compare it to the telephone company's listing. Each time a repairman changes the telephone equipment in your office the detail listing must be corrected. Over a period of time errors occur.

Don't be surprised if you find equipment items on the computer statement which were removed sometime ago but are still being billed in this monthly base charge. Obviously, these erroneous rental charges should be brought to the attention of your telephone company immediately. If you haven't made an inventory of your telephone equipment for some time, there may be a substantial retroactive refund due you for rent which was erroneously charged.

The next step in reducing this base rental charge is to eliminate as much equipment as possible. Start by finding out what is really necessary.

Equipment rates vary widely depending on the type of telephone system you have, the State you are in, and the telephone company which services you. Here is an example of the substantial additional cost that can be incurred for similar service:

John and Mary work in the Accounts Payable Department of the XYZ Company. Each has a single telephone line from the company switchboard. Both employees are sometimes away from their desk visiting other departments. When John is away from his desk Mary reaches over and answers his phone. John also answers Mary's phone when she is absent.

John and Mary have requested new button telephones which will allow them to answer each other's phone at their own desk by having both lines on each phone. This is a simple request for added convenience, but look at the additional cost it generates.

Present System

Two Lines at $5 each	$10.00	
Touch-Tone Charge - 2 x $1	2.00	
Total Cost		$12.00

New System

Two Lines at $5 each	$10.00	
Touch-Tone Charge - 2 x $1	2.00	
Six Button Phones - 2 x $2.75	5.50	
Line Illumination - 2 x $3.00	6.00	
Total Cost		$23.50

Net Additional Cost Per Month	$11.50

Net Additional Cost Per Year	$138.00

In addition there would be an installation charge of $50 or more to make the change.

John and Mary's "simple" change for added convenience would cost more than a week's salary for one of them. Multiply the above by the number of simple requests made each year in a medium size office and you can quickly see how telephone costs can get out of control.

Let's try to satisfy John's and Mary's request for convenience and reduce the cost of their telephone equipment at the same time. In this particular example John and Mary work in the Accounts Payable Department and because of their type of work they make very few phone calls. When the volume of calls is low, often only an extension from the same line is necessary. Thus their request for convenience can be satisfied by simply making Mary's phone an extension of John's line. This change would generate a cost saving as follows:

Cost of Present Equipment		$12.00
Cost of Proposed Equipment		
One Line at $5	$5.00	
Touch-Tone for One Line	1.00	
Cost of Extension	2.50	
Total Cost		$8.50
Net Saving Per Month		$3.50
Net Saving Per Year		$42.00

This cost saving of $3.50 may seem small but it represents a 29% reduction in the monthly cost of the telephone equipment used by these two employees. Had their requested change been made, the cost of their telephone equipment would have increased 96%.

Find out what telephone equipment is really necessary. Then eliminate that equipment which may be nice to have but which is not really needed. You can make a substantial improvement in the monthly base charge on your telephone bill by simply eliminating the unnecessary equipment.

The local telephone company is not the only organization which can furnish your internal telephone equipment. In recent years independent suppliers have been selling larger companies on the economies of owning their own private switchboard and internal equipment. Depending on your particular requirements, privately owned equipment may offer substantial long run savings. A quote from local sales representatives may identify a major cost saving opportunity.

The telephone costs we have discussed thus far are your monthly charges without making any telephone calls. Now, let's look at the costs when you *use* your telephone equipment.

Long Distance and Message Unit Charges

Long distance and message unit charges are based on the *number* of calls made, the *length* of those calls, and the *distance* to the point called. Rates vary widely according to the type of call and the time of day it is placed. Message units apply to calls within your local area where "flat rate" or unlimited trunk lines are not available. In some areas there is a single message unit charge for any local call regardless of its length. In other areas, the distance called may result in multiple message units and after an initial time period, additional message units are charged for overtime.

Many managers are unaware of the extent of message unit charges and feel that by restricting their employee phones to local coverage only, any personal calls which may be made are essentially "free." Not so. These local calls can soon amount to a sizeable additional cost when message units are charged at 6 cents for every five minutes of conversation. These seemingly small charges can often add up to several hundred dollars during a month if you have very many employees.

The best way to eliminate unnecessary message unit charges is to eliminate personal calls. Restrict all telephones to internal calls only for those employees who have no business reason to make outside calls. Unrestricted phones should be kept in locked offices after hours, or should have inexpensive key-operated locks affixed to their dials, to prevent after-hours personnel from using the office telephone system for personal calls. Restricted phones will also help to eliminate long distance personal calling.

Long distance tolls offer the greatest opportunity area for reducing telephone costs. Most cost-conscious managers recognize this potential but are often at a loss to find ways to approach the problem. Since many people cause these costs to be incurred you must get everyone in the office involved. Start with an educational program for all employees which will make them aware of the costs for telephone calls on a per-minute basis. Almost everyone wants to help management reduce costs in this area and any reasonable program is easily sold.

There are three key ways to reduce long distance toll costs; (1) eliminate the need to make as many calls; (2) reduce the length in terms of minutes of necessary calls; and, (3) utilize the lowest rate possible for placing calls. The most effective way to eliminate the number and length of calls is to charge back the cost to the user's department with a detail listing of calls placed. This will help the department managers to review and control the toll costs of their employees. This procedure will effectively eliminate the majority of unnecessary calls and bring to the manager's attention the individuals who tend to be "long talkers." Just bringing excessively long calls to the employees attention can have dramatic effects on a department's monthly toll cost. If further emphasis on the length of calls seems required, there are manufacturers which sell or rent devices that will signal the caller with a "tone" after a preset number of minutes have elapsed.

Placing calls at the lowest rate possible requires considerable understanding on the part of both the manager and his employees. The lowest cost call is one dialed direct without operator assistance. Operator handled calls; such as, those charged to a "third number," collect calls, and credit card calls are always billed at higher rates. Person-to-person calls carry an additional surcharge.

Investigate the operator assisted calls which are charged to your bill and then develop ways for them to be made on a direct dial basis. For example; if salesmen work out of their homes calling customers and charge those calls to your office number, or if they are calling the office collect, have them dial the call direct from their home and submit their home phone bill on their expense report for reimbursement. The difference in cost can be significant.

If there is sufficient volume of collect calls being received from customers, truck drivers, or salesmen, or others who have been authorized to call your office collect, then an inbound WATS or "800" number could be the solution. The main objective is to minimize operator assisted calls and to utilize the lower rates of direct dial calls wherever possible.

Direct dial rates change according to the time of the day the call is placed. Rates are highest during the daytime (8 a.m. to 5 p.m. Monday through Friday), lower in the evenings (5 p.m. to 11 p.m. Monday through Friday and Sunday), and lowest at night and weekends (11 p.m. to 8 a.m. all week, 8 a.m. to 5 p.m. on Sunday and all day Saturday).

How can you benefit from these lower rates? Remember that people in time zones west of you are still working when you're about to go home at 5 p.m. By waiting a minute and placing your call just after 5 p.m., you get a 35% discount.

People in western locations can call east early in the morning and as long as the call is answered before 8 a.m. their time, they can talk all day at a 60% discount. Where branch or sales offices regularly report into the home office the timing of calls with these discount rates in mind can add up to a substantial monthly saving.

How about your customers, do they usually work on Saturdays? Besides receiving a lower telephone rate you may find the man you want has more time available to listen to your sales pitch on Saturdays.

Wide Area Telecommunications Service (WATS)

WATS is a telephone service which offers wholesale rates to long distance telephone users. You can rent a WATS line full-time (24 hours a day, 7 days a week) or on a measured basis (ten hours for a base rental, plus overtime at an hourly rate). Interstate WATS lines vary in cost depending on their coverage. Prices are based on geographical "BANDS" of states, radiating outward from your state. Band coverage is cumulative; thus, a Band 5 WATS line can also be used for calls into Bands 1, 2, 3 and 4. The cost increases with coverage. WATS lines are only one way lines. You can make calls from your office to other locations (outbound); or, you can receive calls from other locations (inbound). Calls within your state require separate intrastate WATS service.

If your office has a sufficient volume of long distance calls it is possible to reduce your cost per call by utilizing WATS lines. But beware, you may find that your *volume* of calls will increase to such an extent that the savings from the lower cost of WATS service is quickly offset.

When WATS lines are installed employees are told to use WATS lines for calls they previously dialed on a toll basis. Often they get the idea that WATS calls are "free." WATS lines are billed on a lump sum basis and since they are not itemized like toll call billings, they are seldom charged back to user departments except on an allocated basis. Unless effective controls are maintained, calls will be made which could have been handled by mail. Also, personal long distance calls increase substantially. As the volume of calls increases, the WATS lines fill up. They are unavailable then when managers need lines to make important business calls. Consequently, overflow is made on a toll basis and new requests are made for additional WATS services. The inevitable result is higher cost.

WATS lines can help to reduce cost; however, the manager must make careful calculations to assure himself that the savings indicated are real. Only by comparing the per-minute cost of your actual pattern of calls with the per-minute cost of the WATS service which covers the same area can you determine if real savings are possible.

Calls must be scheduled and a waiting list is required. The managers in your organization must be willing to wait a reasonable time for access to WATS. If your managers are an impatient group; or, if there are legitimate reasons to make frequent urgent calls, then WATS lines probably won't be cost effective for your operations.

In deciding if WATS service can save toll costs, there are two main considerations to keep in mind; average call length and average call distance. Toll calls cost more for the first minute than for additional minutes. Thus on the first minute or less WATS service is significantly less expensive, but, as the length of your average calls get longer, the advantage of WATS service diminishes. The WATS line rate is the same per minute anywhere within a given Band while toll rates are based on distance. Calls of only a short distance therefore are often less expensive on a toll basis than on WATS. Also, keep in mind that the use of a measured WATS after 5 p.m. and on weekends is more costly than the discounted evening and night rates. For this reason, measured WATS service should not be made available between 5 p.m. and 8 a.m.

After reading the above you may wonder if there is any advantage at all to having WATS service. Often WATS service does not result in overall savings and may very likely increase telephone costs. WATS lines require careful analysis before installation and proper policing after installation. Unless you have sufficient volume to justify a full time WATS line and unless you are able to control and to schedule access to it, WATS service will generally *not* provide sufficient savings to offset the increased volume that having it will generate. Many companies which have WATS would be well advised to remove their present WATS service and re-evaluate their actual need before reconsidering them.

Foreign Exchange Service

Foreign Exchange lines are trunks which effectively put a distance exchange on your switchboard. For example; if your office is located in New York City and you do a substantial portion of your business in Newark, New Jersey, you could arrange to have a Newark, N.J., exchange line tied directly to your office. You would then be able to call within that exchange area on a local call basis and people within that area would be able to call you without incurring a long distance call. A FX line is much like a WATS line except it can be utilized both ways and covers calls only to a specific exchange area. FX lines are subject to the same analysis as WATS lines. They must be justified generally on the basis of customer service and additional sales potential rather than cost reduction objectives.

Getting Assistance to Evaluate Your Telephone Costs

Telecommunications technology has changed rapidly over the past few years. Telephone company rates vary widely between service areas. It is difficult to make a comprehensive evaluation of your telephone needs and costs; however, help is available. The telephone companies have marketing representatives who will assist you without charge to improve the effectiveness of your telephone operations. With their assistance and your own common sense you should be able to make major improvements in telephone costs.

In recent years there have been a number of firms and

individuals who advertise themselves as communications consultants. Their abilities and fees vary widely and it is difficult to evaluate their qualifications. If you decide that you want independent help from a consultant, beware of those who offer their services on a contingent basis and who are not members of a recognized professional association. Remember, you are more familiar with your organization's needs and objectives than a consultant can ever hope to be. A little study and effort on your part will usually be more cost effective in the long run.

Mailing and Postage Costs

Managing mailing and postage costs is a matter of instructing personnel on the "do's" and "don'ts" for increasing or decreasing costs. This is of course an over-simplification but if you will study the following you will understand:

Do:
1. Control the use of stamps.
2. Use metered mail wherever possible.
3. Check postage meters to be sure impressions are legible and do not overlap.
4. Weigh letters carefully for proper postage.
5. Group letters going to the same address, branch office, or customer in one large envelope.
6. Have available the latest postal regulations.
7. Consider size, weight and classes of mail when planning circulars and direct mail advertising pieces.
8. Make certain that business reply cards conform to post office size requirements which qualify for the lowest postage cost.
9. Use seamail, if possible, when pamphlets, brochures, mailing pieces, mats, and similar mail is sent overseas.
10. Consider time versus cost requirements for overseas mail.
11. Use third or fourth class mail when sending supplies and forms to salesmen.
12. Use certified mail rather than registered mail.

13. Replace heavy catalogs with microfilm whenever possible.
14. Be weight conscious when preparing reports.
15. Print intra-company reports on both sides of the paper.
16. Use special light-weight paper for reports that will be mailed.
17. Save unused metered envelopes and tapes for 90% refund at your local post office.
18. Check your mailing scale often.
19. Charge the various departments in your organization for the postage they use.
20. Ask department managers to take steps to reduce postage cost.

Do Not:

1. Send unneeded reports via first class mail.
2. Mail quantities of reports or forms when a single master could be reproduced locally at destination.
3. Mark parcel post packages "special delivery" when "special handling" will get it there as quickly and at lower cost.
4. Send mail Special Delivery on Friday since it probably won't be opened until Monday anyway.
5. Waste postage on mailing lists which need to be updated.
6. Send an invoice separately if it can be included with the package.
7. Use Airmail for domestic mail.
8. Send printed letters, folders, booklets, catalogs, and other similar materials First Class when you qualify for bulk mail savings.
9. Over-pay postage because of inaccurate mailing scales.
10. Fail to have a program and procedures for keeping your mailing lists updated.

Too often little or no management attention is given

to postage costs. With the substantial increases in postage rates, a small amount of management attention in this area could pay handsomely.

Mail Room Operations

In addition to postage savings, an efficiently run mail room can reduce staff and related expenses for inhouse mail preparation and delivery. Here are some questions to use in evaluating the effectiveness of your present mail room, and to reduce its cost of operation.

1. Is your mail room laid out properly so that the mail flows through with the least amount of effort and expenditure of time?

2. Are your mail room operations combined with other functions such as the duplicating department or filing or messenger service so that employees can be utilized for more than one job, thereby reducing costs?

3. Do you measure the mailing task to avoid over-staffing?

4. Could you use staggered shifts or part-time supplementary help to keep permanent staff at a minimum?

5. Is your mailroom used for business mail only or is precious time and efficiency being lost by employees asking to have personal parcels wrapped or envelopes stamped?

6. Should you establish a stringent policy of no wrapping or stamping personal items in the mailroom?

7. Do you require that all personal postage be purchased from a company cashier, petty cash custodian, or a vending machine?

8. Could repetitive chores in the mailroom be improved by automated metering, opening, inserting and wrapping equipment which would speed business mail and free employees for other tasks?

9. Do you have a good postage scale which eliminates overpostage and speeds postage calculations by allowing the correct postage to be read from the scale?

10. When was the last time you checked your present

equipment to see if it's as modern as it should be for your mailing volume?

11. If you have a large volume of outgoing mail, would a machine that folds letters and inserts them and other material into envelopes make the operation more effective?

12. Does your mailroom utilize a mechanical mail opener to assure that incoming mail is opened neatly and quickly without damaging the contents?

13. Do you know what equipment and materials are available free from the U.S. Postal Service to assist your mail room operations?

14. Could you make use of sacks, trays and tags the Postal Service will lend to large mailers?

15. Could you use the dozens of helpful free booklets the Postal Service has available upon request to help business mailers use the mails more profitably?

16. Have you used your Postal Customer Service Representative for assistance in working out your programs for the most efficient and least expensive mail delivery system?

In summary, a little management attention to the average postage costs and mailing activities can uncover cost improvement opportunities which are available for a minimum amount of effort. Take a look at your mailroom practices now.

Office Supplies and Forms Costs

The cost of office supplies and forms is another common office cost which responds well to centralized management. These costs which are incurred by all departments soon get out of control without common standards and direction. To start a cost improvement program in this area, first make someone responsible for overall management and control. Then have that individual take the following steps toward establishing an Office Supplies Control Program.

1. *Standardize Supply Items*

For every department determine the type and quality of each supply item being used and establish the volume of use of each item. Make certain that each item is the most suitable for the use intended. Combine like items used by different departments where possible and establish a standard supply item for those with major volume. Then publish a list of those items which are now considered the company's standard or stock items. Make sure that each department understands which items will be available for requisition from the supply room.

Savings can be effected in your supply room, on your supply purchases, and at inventory time by having as few items as possible in each supply category. For example; study your operations to see how few variants of lead pencil hardness can be stocked and used by all departments, how few kinds of carbon paper and typewriter ribbons are needed, etc. Periodically, review all standard supply items that are being used so that reduction can be made in nonessential items.

2. *Centralize Supply Purchases*

Establish the policy that all purchases will be made by the centralized supply manager who obtains bids from various sources. If individual departments are allowed to do their own purchasing, the advantages of competitive bidding, blanket orders, and centralized control are soon circumvented.

The supply manager should establish minimum and maximum quantities for each standard item based on expected usage. The supplies are then replenished in line with the actual usage, allowing for time required in shipment. He should try to purchase minimum quantities consistent with volume discount prices.

Consider a policy of ordering standard items for a six-month or a one-year period with deliveries being made on a once-a-month basis. This will enable you to get the discount for large quantity purchases. A contract buying program also standardizes the purchases and concentrates the buying power of all offices.

The supply manager should anticipate supply needs and

combine orders so as to minimize time and money expended in writing individual purchase orders.

3. *Centralize Physical Control Over Supplies*

Establish a supply room in a clean, dry area that is enclosed and kept under lock and key. Loss from inadequate storage facilities and careless handling can run high. Provide protected space for storing stationery and other paper supplies. This prevents damage from dust, overcrowding and other types of exposure.

Develop a well thought out system of identifying areas and shelves so that supplies can be located easily. When stocks are replenished, make certain all items are placed on the proper shelves for prompt locating and filling of orders.

Set a "minimum required supply" for each item kept in the stock inventory. Insert a colored card at that point as an automatic reminder to reorder.

Assign stockroom responsibility to specific individuals and don't allow other staff members to enter, browse around, and pick out their own supplies. Free access to supplies provides a temptation for many employees to stock up on items they can conveniently use at home.

4. *Standardize Departmental Requisitioning and Control Procedures*

Set up a system whereby department heads authorize the requisition of supplies. This would provide for a periodic replenishment of supplies rather than a "when needed," day-to-day emergency basis. Arrange for certain departments to place their requests on specific days each week to reduce supply department personnel and eliminate the need for a full time staff.

Provide each department with a steel stationery storage cabinet and there will be no need for daily supply room requests. Give one person in each department the responsibility for ordering and issuing supplies. Eliminate local pilferage of supplies by establishing physical controls similar to those in the main supply room; i.e., permit only certain pre-selected individuals access to supply cabinets. Route *all* requisitions for supplies, even those not normally stocked, through the centralized supply manager. If there are enough requests for a new item, it may be decided to start stocking it.

Establishing a Forms Control Program

The cost of forms in many companies is a major expense. A comprehensive examination of those forms will usually indicate two major problems; (1) Too many different types; and, (2) A need to upgrade and increase the effectiveness of those needed.

Often an improved design will result not only in a reduction of cost of the form itself, but will also reduce the required preparation time.

To develop these improvements a Forms Control Program should be established. There are advantages to having the same individual who is responsible for office supplies, also be in charge of your Forms Control Program. Forms are, in a broad sense, a supply item which can be integrated into Centralized Purchasing, Physical Controls, and Standardized Requisitioning Procedures already discussed.

The standardization and combining of forms can really pay off in lower staffing costs and reduced processing cycles. The following steps should be taken to set up an effective Forms Control Program:

1. Standardize and Improve Current Forms in Use

Collect all of the forms that are currently being used in your office and be sure that you get every last one. Check with all departments. Ask the Purchasing Department for their records on what forms were purchased in the last year and make inquiries of branch offices. After you have made certain that you have all of these forms, prepare an index and classify the various forms by use and department. Then prepare a summary sheet and attempt to simplify or combine some of the various forms and eliminate others. It is a rare company that doesn't have forms that are duplicated, as well as those with similar information which can be combined.

Start by asking if all the forms are really necessary. Some forms are prepared and distributed only because no one has ever taken the trouble to check whether or not they have retained their usefulness over the years. Changing conditions might have eliminated the need for some that are still being made up regularly as a matter of routine and inertia. Prepare a questionnaire; ask each originator and recipient for his evaluation of the importance of the form. There is no sense in trying to improve something that should simply be eliminated in the first place.

Now, review the design of each form. Forms should be standardized to ensure best use of space and logical work flow sequence of entries. Discuss the use and purpose of each form with those who use them. A form should contain a specific amount and kind of information. All unnecessary information should be eliminated. A well designed form should be prepared so that it is easy to enter the information on it. The horizontal lines should not be too narrow and vertical lines properly placed. Test out the form to see that it follows the normal spacing of a typewriter.

Make sure that the forms are so organized as to make essential information immediately visible to those who examine them for vital data. Determine the two or three items that are the most important information on each form and set them off with boxes, color, arrows or some other attention getting device. The supplementary information on each form is usually there for supporting purposes, but it should not interfere with the user's ability to spot essential information quickly.

The format as well as the content of a much used form can often be altered to effect savings. Even the lining up of certain blanks might well result in eliminating excess spacing motions by typists.

If any form is used in conjunction with others, similar information on each should be listed in the same order.

This speeds up the filing in process and minimizes possibilities of error.

Also examine the forms from the standpoint of the paper stocks used. If some or all can be printed on paper of the same color and weight, savings in paper buying will result. For accuracy and simplification of distribution, consider standard paper colors for form carbons and originals.

Review the various forms as to ease of use. For example: time spent in inserting carbons between copies of forms to be filled in on the typewriter can be saved by the use of specially printed forms with carbons already interlaced or printed right on carbon-backed sheets.

Analyze the printed forms you are using to see whether their respective sizes and the quantities regularly used make it possible to print several different forms in one operation thus saving on individual print run costs. Sometimes a slight change in the overall size of one or more forms can make this possible.

As you review each form, keep in mind that printing paper comes in certain standard sizes. Much stock can be wasted if the size of your form does not cut out efficiently from a standard sheet.

As you can see there are many things to consider in the design of forms, to increase their effectiveness, and to minimize their cost. Large companies have found that it pays them to have a forms design expert on their permanent staff. Smaller companies can get help in many cases from their forms supplier who has had wide experience in the design of many types of forms.

After you have done everything possible to standardize, combine, eliminate, and improve the forms in use, establish a listing of standard approved forms. Each form should be given a number for easy reference and identification, as well as an official title.

Establish a hard and fast rule that no new forms can be prepared unless the form design is approved by the Forms Manager.

2. *Standardize Purchasing Practices for Forms*

If you use many different forms, each in quantity, run a cost study to determine the best method of reproduction. You may even find, as some firms have, that it will pay you to set up your own printing and reproduction department.

If you continue to have at least some of your forms printed by outside suppliers, prepare the copy carefully with complete specifications. Forms are usually tailormade. If the forms are needed in a hurry, the usual case, the printer must know precisely what you need. You, and not the printer, should determine the final design of the form.

Ask for bids on each job. Some purchasing agents ask for bids only occasionally because of their relationship with printers who have done good work in the past. This appears to save time and effort, but the company does not always get the lowest cost printing this way. A printer may submit a low bid on the occasional bid job and then find he has to make up for it by higher prices on the non-bid printing that follows.

Lump small orders together before asking for bids. A little tighter control over form ordering will usually make it possible to get a single bid for a group of forms, resulting in lower unit costs.

Buy in the largest quantity possible. However, forms that are apt to become obsolete quickly should be bought in small quantities; even with the higher cost it is cheaper than scrapping an entire inventory.

Your printers have other customers beside you. Ask them to let you know whenever they are running a job for someone else on which a saving can be effected by running it with one of your own forms. If the color of the stock and ink are identical with those of the other customer, and if the quantities needed are fairly equal, you may be able to take advantage of the press run to obtain a stock of forms at a lower cost.

Avoid the excessive costs incurred for overtime and rush work resulting from last minute emergency orders of forms that have run out. Estimate your long range supply need, and have your printer run whatever quantity is needed to maintain that number of sheets in stock every time you pick up a supply from him.

Unless you are familiar with printing costs and current prices, stay away from long-term printing contracts with a single printer. The contract method saves time and paperwork, but will keep you from realizing savings from lower bidders.

Make certain that you receive the forms you pay for. Bids often vary as much as 100%, but the lowest bid is not always the best one. The cost of using a form runs as high as eight times the price of the form. The loss in clerical time and errors resulting from the use of poor forms may be more than the "savings" on bids.

A Forms Control Program is an effective way to reduce the cost of office operations in all departments. Most companies who have established such a program have realized substantial cost savings.

Other Common Office Costs

Space does not permit a detail discussion of all the various common office costs which offer cost improvement opportunities. The centralized overall Cost Management Approach discussed for telephones, postage, and supply costs can also be effectively applied to other office costs. Sometimes it's a matter of looking at office costs from a different perspective. For example; when was the last time you considered the possible advantages of centralizing some office functions?

Engineering, Accounting, Administration and Industrial Relations are only some of the functions which can be centralized to achieve substantial advantages. Reduced costs and improved control can be a substantial advantage for considering centralization. Managers change and different circumstances evolve with time. Periodic reviews of your company organization can identify significant reasons for centralization of office functions. Unless you have re-evaluated your mode of operation recently, you may find a change could produce significant cost improvements.

The use of computers in office operations is another area that can point out cost improvement opportunities by using a different perspective. The following five questions are examples of looking at this cost from a different angle.

1. *Are you over-using computers?*

In the rush to computerize operations some companies have put various systems on their computer which never should have been mechanized. Low volume or exception prone systems can often be done by other methods at less cost. Good manual systems can be cost savers if properly implemented and controlled. Because of competition and available computer time, many banks are selling payroll preparation services that are more cost effective than company owned systems.

If you haven't made a complete review of the cost of your computerized systems and compared them to the various alternatives recently, you might find such a review extremely profitable.

2. *Would it pay you to buy a used computer?*

Because of the rapid technology change which has taken place in the computer industry there are many used computers on the market at very attractive prices. If you are considering renting a computer or adding capacity to existing equipment, it may save you money to buy one of these older models. Many times certain selected work can be run on older and slower equipment at substantially less additional cost than adding new capacity.

3. *Is your computer under a "third party lease?"*

Most companies simply lease their computer equipment from the manufacturer. Many leasing companies, however, will buy your present equipment and lease it to you at substantially reduced rates. Often these "third party leases" have the same cancellation clause as the original lease. Maintenance would still be available from the manufacturer.

4. Have you considered selling computer time to other companies?

As companies grow they may need to install larger computer capacity in order to provide for future growth, or to obtain special features that are only available on larger equipment. Selling excess computer time to other companies, who need computer time either because of a temporary situation or because they are not large enough to have their own computer, can substantially reduce data processing fixed overhead. Some companies have also found they can sell their Systems and Programming Expertise at rates which will give them not only recovery of overhead but profit as well.

5. Have you considered the new mini-computers?

New small computers affectionately called "Mini-Computers" have been introduced by a number of manufacturers. These small computers are capable of doing most of the routine applications which are done on larger ones except they operate slower and cost substantially less. Some versions costing less than $500 per month will do the work of several clerks, and will double as an automatic typewriter and teletype machine. Many larger companies are finding that mini-computers are more economical at their smaller locations than their large centralized installations. Most of the mini-computers can also be used as remote input stations for larger jobs which must be processed on the larger centralized equipment.

The first four questions above could also be asked about other office equipment; such as office copiers, for instance.

Look at each and every one of your office costs. Then use your imagination to develop ways to eliminate or reduce these costs. For example, do you spend a substantial amount on advertising? Then maybe you should have your own advertising agency. An accredited agency gets a 15% commission which many times is enough to pay the salary of a full time manager as well as show a profit. With your company's advertising as a base, a small agency is then in a position to take on some outside clients without much additional overhead, and thus again increase profits.

Make a summary listing of your company's various office costs. Now go down the list and develop cost improvement ideas for each category of expense. Ask the assistance of other managers and your employees. Surprisingly, wild ideas can often turn into substantial cost savings. In the next chapter we will discuss several ways to develop cost improvement ideas of this kind.

9 DEVELOPING COST IMPROVEMENT IDEAS

Every business operation, regardless of its size or nature, is faced with a variety of operating problems which are causing unnecessary costs. If you have analyzed and evaluated your operations as we discussed in previous chapters, then you have no doubt identified a large list of cost generating problems. Your ability to turn these problems into opportunities by implementing cost improvement ideas could mean the difference between success or failure as an effective manager, and in some cases of the financial future of your company.

Personal success enjoyed by many managers in business is a direct result of cost improvement ideas developed for their employers. The identification of opportunities, development of ideas, and implementation of programs which improve profits bring increases in salary, promotions, and other forms of recognition.

To a very substantial extent, every manager's business and personal development, growth as a professional manager, and personal economic well-being depends on his ability to develop ideas which increase the effectiveness and profitability of his operations.

With that thought in mind, let's look at some of the ways which have been found to be helpful in turning operational problems into ideas for increasing profits.

The Time for Developing Cost Improvement Ideas

To develop cost improvement ideas means you must take time to *think*.

Most managers are too busy with the day-to-day business problems to think about improving profits. Don't be like the rest of the crowd. Provide time for thinking about your operations as well as time to do the necessary planning to improve them. "Time," you say, "that's the one thing I never seem to have enough of." If you think about it, you have the same amount of time as everyone else. Everybody has twenty-four hours a day. Some people just seem to make better use of their time than others. You are probably wasting your time on unimportant day-to-day activities while the big opportunities for cost improvements pass you by.

But what will others think if you take time to plan, time to develop a more effective approach to managing your operations? If you tell them you are developing your cost management abilities and capabilities they are apt to say "no one is paid to sit around learning to be capable of achievement."

Since there is no way of evaluating such capability, companies pay and promote according to visible achievement. Many managers feel it is far better to work diligently using the same old losing approach (even one that is recognized as being wrong) to impress their superiors with their industriousness than to sit around pondering a better solution. To them it would be even worse to admit they don't know a winning solution. It may well be that the manager who is sitting around thinking is far closer to the most profitable answer. How can such a thing be judged until his approach is actually implemented and the achievement of the objective becomes visible? By the final long term results of his operations.

In the long run it is far more profitable to have managers who plan their moves to achieve the right objective than to have managers busily achieving lesser objectives. But are there companies who are willing to invest the time to develop a different approach on the mere possibility that it will be more profitable? At this writing most companies adhere to a system that does not afford time to think and plan a long-range approach to cost management. If you are being pressured by such attitudes simply ask, "Can they afford the non-progress of not providing the planning time?"

Yes, you must provide time to develop your thoughts and formulate an overall plan. One man I know arrives early at the office but will not accept any phone calls or interruptions for the first hour. This is his thinking time, at the beginning of the day when his mind is fresh and alert to ponder the major problems and to develop solutions.

Regardless of pressures not to take time to think things through, you must make the necessary time even at the expense of delaying other less important activities.

Each person's mind operates on a different time basis. Select a time period when you feel most comfortable about digging into the major opportunities in your operations. Some people prefer the early morning hours while others feel that they don't get rolling until later in the day. Analyze yourself and determine when is best for you and then set aside that period for your thinking and developing hours.

Your Place for Developing Ideas

Almost as important as time, is having a place for solving problems and developing cost improvement ideas.

Some people are able to do this type of in-depth thinking at work, but often there are too many interruptions there. Between telephone calls, appointments and questions from subordinates, the day is too broken up to concentrate on the creative thinking needed to develop cost improvement ideas.

As with time, the place will be different for each individual. Some managers find their best ideas coming to mind as they drive to work. For those individuals I suggest a small tape recorder or dictation machine for verbal notes that can be transcribed later.

Other individuals find they think best in their favorite easy chair in the living room, while shaving in the morning, in bed at night just before they go to sleep, a rocker on the patio, or whatever place seems to relax the mind so that the subconscious can start releasing ideas it has been working on without your realizing it.

I prefer a little study I set up in my home. I sometimes go there after dinner for an hour or so, or wake up early in the morning unable to sleep because my mind is full of ideas. I find those early morning hours in my study the most productive. In earlier years (when I was working in New York,) I found my most productive place was on the commuter train during the hour ride to and from the city. I would try to get a seat by the window where I wouldn't be disturbed, then I would pull out my pad and pencil while others were busy reading their newspapers.

Make a start now by jotting down what might be your best places for developing cost improvement ideas. Don't limit yourself to only one specific place. Ideas can pop up almost anytime, so be prepared.

The key items to have are a pad and a pencil. Write your ideas down the moment they come to you. The brain sometimes spills out a string of creative ideas in a fast chain reaction. One idea leading to another, and another. You must be just as quick to write them down, or they will be gone forever. Often you will be unable to recall an idea which is lost from that first fleeting moment it comes to you.

So, select a place that seems to be best for you to develop cost improvement ideas and spend as much time there as you find you need to stimulate the flow of ideas from your mind.

Ways to Develop Ideas

There are many ways to develop your cost improvement ideas. Here are a few that are practiced by successful managers.

1. Look at Weaknesses

One way to get the flow of cost improvement ideas started is to list what appears to be presently inadequate. Then list all the possible ways you can improve or strengthen the weakness.

How do you find out what those weaknesses are? Ask the user of the end product. For example, let's say you are trying to improve packaging costs. You feel they are too high but need ideas on how to lower them. Ask the packing supervisor what he feels are weaknesses with the current packaging materials. He may tell you that they don't work well on the present packing machinery, causing jam ups and destroying material.

Ask the shipping supervisor. He may tell you that current materials do not protect the product adequately in shipment, that they cause excessive breakage and consequent returns from customers.

Ask your customers and you may find that the packaging is causing them problems in storage or excessive material handling.

Now take this list and develop ways to correct these weaknesses. Your solutions may not reduce the actual cost of packaging but could substantially reduce packing labor, shipping breakage, and customer dissatisfaction. Often what appears to be the problem will lead you to a long list of other areas where potential savings from cost improvements are even greater.

This same approach can be used for developing improved procedures in any area of the business. Ask the user, whether the end product is a report, commission check, or a supply item you furnish someone else in the organization, and he can tell you what is wrong and often how to improve it. Maybe the report is inaccurate, gives too much or too little usable information, or is not received on time to be as valuable as it could be.

When a commission check is incorrect or not received promptly the salesman who receives it will probably let you know without having to ask him. What you have to ask is his suggestion on how to eliminate the problem. Maybe it could be mailed directly to his bank to speed up delivery.

Users of operating supplies may be wondering why you

are furnishing such a cheap brand supply item which is causing extra labor time to do the job, but they probably won't tell you unless you make it a point to ask.

So, start with the weaknesses your reviews have uncovered, but also follow through to the end user and find out all the weaknesses and suggested solutions before you try to solve the problem.

2. *Look at the good features*

Can you capitalize on aspects of your operations, or are they really needed? This is the opposite approach from looking at weaknesses. Let's take the packing cost example again. When you talk to the packing supervisor he may laud the material being used as the toughest he's ever seen; so tough in fact that the cutting blades on the packing equipment have to be changed more frequently. The shipping supervisor may tell you that they seldom have any breakage problem, "They use so much cushion around the product that we simply kick them off the truck when we get to the customer." The customer may reply to your question by stating that, "Your boxes are so good we reuse them to ship our products."

All this praise should lead you to the conclusion that you may be "overpackaging." Can a new package be designed that isn't as tough, doesn't cushion the product as well, isn't such a bargain for the customer, but would cost a lot less?

Looking at good features may point out that the cost of those features do not warrant their continuation. On the other hand, if the cost saving is minimal, can you capitalize on those good features? Can you increase packing speed with this tough material which doesn't cause the machine to break down or jam? Can you get a lower freight rate because of its durability in shipment? Can you use the customer's goodwill in your sales approach to other customers?

Good features may cost more than the benefits they provide; or, they may not be utilized to the fullest. A list of these good features can point out many ways to improve costs.

Look at all your procedures and methods the same way. That extra, unused information in a report may not cost much to present, but the cost of gathering and summarizing it could be substantial. High priced supply items can be replaced with less expensive substitutes which work just as well without any loss of efficiency.

3. Break down the operation into smaller parts and evaluate each segment.

This is a divide and conquer method. A problem which is hard to nail down, often is easier to understand and solve when you concentrate on smaller areas first and then put it all together in your final solution.

Looking at the total procurement cycle of a business can be an overwhelming task. Yet it needs to be done in many companies. If you break the review down into manageable segments such as the requisitioning, purchasing, receiving and accounts payable functions, you can then review each of the operations separately and develop many ways to improve each. Each segment can also be broken down into the various activities necessary to accomplish it. Purchasing for example can be broken down as follows:

1. Reviewing the requisition to determine that the item to be purchased is fully detailed as to specifications, requirements, anticipated use, etc.
2. Selecting the best supplier based on quality, delivery, price, reliability, and payment terms.
3. Placing the order, usually a clerical activity, but what many people mistakenly think is the purchasing department's primary function.
4. Expediting and following up to see that the requisitioned item is delivered in accordance with the required delivery date.

Purchasing departments have many other activities but the four listed generally represent the major ones. Each of these is often a separate group within a large purchasing department and can be broken down further into the specific procedures followed by each group. Evaluating any operational cycle within a company can be a major undertaking but when it is broken down into smaller segments it is more easily understood. Improvements listed for each of the smaller segmented activities can then be put back together into one overall action plan.

4. *Can you simplify it?*

If you have ever met an IBM salesman, no doubt sometime during your discussions he has referred to K.I.S. *Keep It Simple.* Computers are really very simple. It is people who consider them to be complex. They operate on the principle that a switch is either "on" or "off." A point in their memory is either minus or plus. Pictures are simply a mass of dots which are either black or white. How much simpler can something be?

It's the fantastic speeds at which they manipulate these plus or minus, on or off, and black or white points that enable a computer to do so many things that are not humanly possible. The "simple-minded" computer must be told what to do in very detailed terms. These detailed instructions are called a program. When activities are to be put on a computer the actual development of the program results in understanding which enables the steps in a given procedure to be substantially reduced.

Don't wait until your procedures get so complex that you need a computer to do them. Simplify them now. First, break the problem down into simple steps, then, set down ways to simplify these steps. Eliminate the unnecessary ones just as a programmer does when he prepares the logic for a computer program. The process of making a simple flow chart of a procedure will often lead to cost improvement ideas. Then take the simplified steps and put them back together into the simplest procedure which will accomplish the task required. Keep in mind that the simplest way is usually the best.

5. *Adapt and apply solutions from similar problems.*

This related-experience approach is perhaps one of the most common. All managers have had some experience at solving various problems. Applying a previous solution to a similar situation is done by most without even thinking about it. Without giving the problem some concentrated thought we are apt to pick the first similar solution which comes to mind. Try instead to list the main criteria of the situation. Then jot down similar problems you have experienced and recall how you solved them. Last but most important, find out how other companies have handled similar situations. Keep in mind that your experience is limited. Don't be reluctant to use someone else's approach if it's better than anything you have tried. When it comes to business methods, most companies are happy to share with others. Most trade journals contain a wealth of information on how other companies have reduced their costs.

Now, look over your list and see whether you can adapt any of the potential answers to your current problem. You may find that parts of several, when put together, will give you an even better solution.

Cost conscious managers are continually exposing themselves to how others run their operations. They continually search for new ideas they can apply to their operations. Subscribe to business magazines in your field and study them. Don't hesitate to buy and read the latest books available on cost improvement techniques. One good idea that can be adapted to your operations will pay the price of the book many times over. Try to learn something new and different every day. You never know when that method you learned today, which does not immediately apply to your operations, will spark an adaptation that will solve a major problem for you tomorrow.

6. *Adapt and apply solutions from dissimilar problems.*

Many ideas can be adapted or copied from unrelated fields. This can best be explained by giving the following example:

A controller at a large manufacturing plant was faced with developing a system for controlling the issuance and use of shop supplies. The plant had more than four hundred foremen and supervisors who were authorized to requisition supplies for approximately 5,000 employees. A formal requisitioning system was supposed to be in effect. This system required the foremen to approve in writing all supplies issued from the central warehouse, but it was virtually impossible to hold the warehouse men responsible for proper issues or the foremen for supplies requisitioned in their names. With so many authorized signers and a constant turnover of personnel, recognition of authorized signatures was at best a guess. It was impractical to hold the foremen responsible for usage of supplies, because there was no easy way to account for the actual amount of supplies issued to a given foreman. Many of the supplies were low in value per unit, therefore an elaborate, costly procedure was not practical. The cost of supplies purchased was simply allocated to each foreman's cost center based on the number of manhours worked in his department. The annual cost of supplies being allocated in this manner totalled over a half million dollars. Needless to say, this was a sizable expenditure being made with no assigned responsibility for its control. Except for indirect labor supervised by each of the foremen, supplies represented the largest single overhead category. A system was needed which would motivate their attention and efforts to control this cost.

Every system that came to mind was either too costly or too cumbersome to be practical. Then one day on a trip to the home office, the controller was looking through one of the airline magazines which had many advertisements for credit cards. An idea came to mind. Why not issue a credit card to each foreman for use as identification and authority to requisition supplies. Would it work? A further appealing idea was the connotation in the minds of people that a credit card results in charges to their account. After all, wasn't each foreman's budget his account against which he could charge a certain amount of supplies?

When the idea was discussed with the systems department, they sketched out a three part requisition form similar to that used by many credit card systems. The first copy would be retained by the foreman as his record of the items he requisitioned, much like the customer copy of a credit card form. The second copy would serve as a dray ticket for delivering the supplies from the warehouse to the shop floor, and the third copy would be the source document which could be coded and used for the computer to update inventory records and provide the needed control reports.

The local bank was asked where they got the card imprinters. They said that they had a large supply left over and would be happy to supply the twenty or so which were needed. They also provided information about the purchase of plastic cards and agreed to provide their equipment to prepare the cards for use. The shop superintendents liked the idea.

Within 60 days the new requisition system was implemented. The results were amazing. The first year the system was in use supply costs were reduced by 40%.

There are probably many applications where this credit card idea could be applied in your business to help control costs. It is presented here only as an example of how you can adapt and apply solutions from dissimilar situations to improve your operations.

Idea-Starter Words

Sometimes a checklist of key words will trigger a new idea which will solve an operating problem. Here are some that have been used to improve operational procedures and methods. You may want to make up your own list of key words after you have studied the following:

1. *Adaptation*: Can a concept that works well in another area be adapted and used to solve this problem?
2. *Addition*: Can something be added to improve the situation? More attention, effort, staffing, etc. Con-

versely, can something be subtracted to make improvement?

3. *Association*: How is this problem associated with others in the procedure? If the other problem is solved perhaps this one would be eliminated.

4. *Combination*: Can this be combined with something else? Everything, from simple steps in a procedure to whole departments, can be subjected to combinations which streamline operations and reduce costs.

5. *Elimination*: Can this operation or function be eliminated entirely? How about eliminating part of it? Is it really needed?

6. *Opposition*: Who opposes it and why? What suggestions has he offered to solve it?

7. *Replacement*: Can the entire method be replaced with something better? How many times have you tried without success to improve something only to end up replacing it completely?

8. *Reversal*: Can we perform the procedure in reverse order? Paint the product before assembly or assemble it before we paint it.

9. *Timing*: Would a change in timing improve costs? Bringing in supplies earlier or later; speeding up work flow; cycle billing customer accounts, etc.

10. *Substitution*: Can materials, equipment, supplies be substituted which cost less but work as well?

Make up your own list of idea-starter words then go over it each time you tackle a new problem. You might want to place your list of idea-starter words nearby—on your desk, on the wall, or in your pocket. In that way it will be a handy prod for your mind when you really need an idea. Better yet, memorize these checkpoints; get to know them so well they become a built-in part of your brain. When a problem needs solving, ideas will emerge much faster under the stimulus of these points. With a little practice you will find that this approach will start a whole flow of ideas. Jot them down no matter how foolish they sound at first. Sometimes the best solution comes from an unusual idea which sounded crazy when first proposed.

Developing Your Own Methods

These are examples of different methods which have been found to be helpful in developing cost improvement ideas. Any or all of them can be used to spur your mind into action. Sooner or later, as you practice your cost conscious skills, you will of course find yourself developing your own methods.

Just as no two person's fingerprints are identical, no two managers are identical in terms of their knowledge, understanding, attitudes, weaknesses, and abilities. Each must develop his own method of getting ideas out of his mind and into a usable form.

The purpose of explaining some of the methods used by the author is simply to stimulate and inspire you to create your own special system for producing a quantity of cost improvement ideas. By all means try those suggested here and if they work for you, continue to use them. In the long run, however, you will probably feel more comfortable if you adopt your own approach.

Summary

Cost improvement ideas are funny things; they don't work unless implemented, and the harder you work on their implementation, the greater the results. The basic idea isn't as important as what you do with it; in fact, the idea doesn't even have to be original. Some of the author's best cost improvements had been used before by other companies. There aren't many really original ideas; most which we think as original are merely a fresh approach of applying an old technique.

Your best ideas will usually pop up when you are stocking your mind with a basic understanding of what is happening around you. If you never take the time to look around, you will probably rush right by hundreds of potentially profitable ideas. Since cost improvement ideas are everywhere, the obvious dangers are identification or confusion in trying to organize them into workable programs and projects.

In choosing ideas for cost improvement: (a) be selective and discriminating, choosing ideas which will have the greatest effect on bottom-line profits; (b) concentrate on ideas with which you can identify or that interest you; (If you don't *feel* a deep involvement in your idea or project, how can you expect your subordinates or those around you to want to get involved and assist you with its implementation?); (c) don't hide your improvement ideas from others; if it is really as good as it seems, it will stand up under severe criticism. In fact, by discussing a good idea with others, it will usually improve with further scrutiny and evaluation. You also get the benefit of another's thoughts and experience.

Cost improvement ideas can sometimes be so complex they literally stagger the imagination and, conversely, ideas so simple you wonder why they never occurred to someone else long before you were faced with solving the problem. The size or uniqueness of the idea is unimportant, having the right idea at the right time is what counts.

10 STEPS FIVE AND SIX

Throughout the preceding pages we have discussed many ways to analyze and evaluate your operations in order to identify cost improvement opportunities. We have also discussed ways to develop cost improvement ideas to exploit these opportunities. However, the best ideas in the world are of little value until action is taken to convert your ideas into tangible savings. No book can show you what action to take, or when to take it. You and you alone must make the final decision. You must set the wheels in motion to convert your ideas into action programs to obtain the desired results.

If you jotted down notes as you read the preceding pages, then no doubt you have several potential cost improvements already formulated which can be acted upon immediately. Do something about them now. By tomorrow some other operating problem may fill your mind and today's ideas will be set aside and forgotten.

Take Action Now—Convert Your Ideas Into Action

No cost improvement program can give lasting effects unless such a program is a continuing one. It must also involve as many employees as possible. In order to have as many employees as possible involved, there must first be a program to develop a cost awareness at all levels. Top management is very much aware of the need for improving profit through lower costs. At the Middle Management level this cost consciousness is obscured because of their proximity to the daily operating problems. Supervisors at the next level of management often have such a limited view of the overall operation that the development of the cost conscious attitude becomes exceedingly difficult. At the employee level, cost awareness is hardest to develop. There is little motivation to save the large impersonal company money when there is no expectation of any personal benefits by the employee. How then does one get everyone involved in an effective and continuing cost improvement program?

Start at the top by getting strong support from top management. This is usually the easiest step since most top management is actively seeking the benefits that can be derived from a successful cost management program.

Next, develop an atmosphere at the middle management level which fosters achievement with recognition and reward. Involve middle management to the greatest extent possible in the development of the overall company goals. Make them a part of the company's objectives; have them develop objectives and programs for their operations which can be directly related to the overall company objectives.

Budgets and financial plans are excellent tools with which to project and monitor progress at this level. To be successful a cost management program must develop a cost conscious attitude among those in middle management.

Encourage middle managers to solicit cooperation in the cost management program from their supervisors. Urge them to keep the cost implications of every decision continually in the forefront. When supervisors continually see the effect of their actions in terms of cost they will begin to develop the cost conscious attitude. Strengthen this development through recognition of any cost saving idea or action, no matter how small. Try, if possible, to make the recognition tangible. Picking up the lunch check for a supervisor that just came up with a cost saving idea may seem like a minimal reward, but it is a tangible recognition he can understand and appreciate. Discuss his contributions to the cost improvement program when you reveiw his progress or give him a raise. Associate the idea of cost improvement with promotions, salary increases, and other forms of recognition.

Encourage your supervisors to solicit cooperation and ideas from other employees. Set up definite programs to solicit ideas and cultivate a cost improvement atmosphere in every department.

Involve your supervision in detail reviews of their operations, such as those discussed in Chapter 4 of this book. Have books like this available for them to read and study. Don't do these things on a one time basis, but regularly, each time a new problem arises, or a new opportunity for cost improvement presents itself.

The key for a successful continuing cost management program is:

Continuing Involvement and Recognition

11 PARTING WORDS

We have come a long way since we started in the first chapter. We have covered a great many approaches to identifying improvements and have discussed a great many ideas that could help improve the cost of your operations.

It isn't necessary that you agree with everything that has been said here or that all the ideas are adaptable to your operations. The main objective has been to stimulate your thinking about ways to manage the costs in your operations more effectively.

It is important to realize that your operations have the potential to be more cost effective, that you can discover and develop the ideas to make them more profitable, and that only you can take the action necessary to make it all happen. No book could ever cover every possible idea for cost improvement any more than it could list every question you should ask about your operations.

Examine your attitude carefully. The importance of the first step of the Cost Management Approach; i.e., the developing of a Cost Management Attitude cannot be stressed strongly enough. Without it your eyes will not be fully opened to the opportunities which surround you.

Know and practice every day the following principles of a good Cost Management Program:

1. Management and individual managers must have or must develop a Cost Conscious attitude. An effective

cost management program must have the strong support of top management and this attitude must be reflected by department managers and supervisors in order to permeate down to everyone in the organization.

2. Costs must be managed by those responsible for the incurrence of them. Others in the organization can influence and give assistance. However, cost improvements must be made where costs are incurred. The influence that lower level supervisors have over costs is amazingly significant.

3. Costs must be known and understood before they can be managed. If managers and supervisors do not know what their costs are or how their actions affect the costs in their department or company, they can hardly be expected to develop better ways to control them.

4. Individuals must be motivated to improve costs. Incentives which motivate vary from the firing of a manager if he doesn't improve costs to the other extreme of gifts, awards and bonuses. The most powerful incentive is recognition, which can vary from a pat on the back to monetary rewards. Regardless of how it is accomplished, a good cost management program must motivate, and encourage the cooperation of all persons to improve costs.

5. To be effective and to have any lasting benefits, a cost management program must be accomplished through your existing overall organization. Consultants, audit teams, or special committees accomplish temporary cost reductions, but long term improvements require continuing vigilance. A committee or other group may be helpful to plan and coordinate the program, but the organization as a whole must contribute and build the program into their daily operations to obtain lasting results. The most effective programs have the coordinated efforts of all departments within the company.

6. Cost improvements are achieved through creative thinking and innovative development of better ways to accomplish the objectives of the organization. This imaginative approach must be applied to all areas; such as, new product designs, new selling techniques, new manufactur-

ing processes, new procedural methods, new organizational structures, etc. No area in the company should be excluded and all employees should be encouraged to participate. The collective thinking of all can be a powerful resource for a company to utilize.

7. Methods, procedures, and cost improvements should be gleaned from every source available. Don't fail to borrow ideas from other companies, other industries, or other individuals. Consider ways that are opposite, similar, dissimilar, complete changes, etc. Don't restrict your thinking with preconceived ideas or notions. Keep your mind and the minds of your employees open to all possible ways of solving cost problems. Encourage interchange of ideas with others, researching to find ideas in books, magazines, and other sources. A simple, sometimes novel idea which may seem wild at first, may later prove to be the very profitable answer.

Create an atmosphere which will foster and support these principles each day in every action you take as a manager and your continuing cost management program will succeed.

The opportunities for cost management in business today are unending. The men or women who master the Cost Management Approach will be valuable members of the management team, for they will have found the true potential of their operations.

INDEX

A

ABC Method
 For inventory, 108
 Labor content, 122
 Purchased components, 118-119
Accounts Receivable
 Capital in, 102
 Cash discounts, 103-104
 Credit approvals, 104
 Credit & collection, 102-103
 Credit memos, 103
 Uncollectable, 104-105
Action, need to take, 185
Activity list
 Form, 62
 Instructions, 61-66
Advertising, 169
Advisors
 Telephone Company, 156
 U.S. Postal Service, 160
Air freight, 136-137
Anticipating problems, 90-91
Appraisal, of performance, 92-93
Atmosphere
 Cultivating for cost improvement,
  43-44
 Department, 87-88
Attitude
 Managers about costs, 21-29
 The cost conscious, 27-29
 Toward other departments, 96
Awareness
 Manager of budget, 93-94
 Employee, 94-95

B

Bank services, 102
Bids, competitive for
 Forms, 166-167
 Office supplies, 161
 Transport services, 136
Bills of lading, 137
Budgets, 93-94

C

Cash
 Balances, 99-100
 Borrowed, 101
 Discounts, 103-104
 Number of accounts, 100
 Zero balance accounts, 100
Competitive bids
 Forms, 166-167
 Office supplies, 161
 Transport services, 136
Computers
 Mini-computers, 169
 Over-using, 168
 Selling time, 169
 Should you buy, 168
 Third party leases, 168
Conditioning thinking, 72-73
Consolidating shipments, 136
Consultants
 Management, 59
 Telephone, 156-157
Containers
 Effect on freight rates, 137
 Re-use of, 138

Coordinator, Staffing review, 60
Cost
  Avoidance, 36-37
  Categories, 75-76
  Directly visible, 71
  Elimination, 38-39
  Forms, 163-167
  Importance of, 21-24
  Improvement, 72
  Indirect labor, 140-142
  Indirect materials, 142-143
  Indirectly visible, 71-72
  Mailing & postage, 157-160
  Maintenance, 143-144
  Management, 15, 40-41
  Office supplies, 160-163
  Other overhead, 144-145
  Prevention, 37-38
  Reduction, 15, 39-40
  Salary, 139-140
  Standard, 114-117
  Telephone, 147-157
Cost conscious attitude
  Chart, 30
  Developing a, 29-32
Cost conscious manager, 32-34
Cost improvement atmosphere, 43-44
Cost management
  Ability development, 43-44
  Definition, 40-41
  Program principles, 189-191
Credit memos, 103
Cross training, 92
Copy machines, 169

D
Data processing (See Computers)
Delegation, 83-84
Deliveries
  Call ahead, 138
  Office supplies, 161
Department
  Atmosphere, 87-88
  Goals, 79
Designing
  Office forms, 164-165
  Organization, 95

Developing cost improvement
  Ideas, 171-184
  Time for, 173-174
  Ways to, 174-181
Direct labor
  Standards, 120-121
  Simplified measuring, 121-122
  Working smarter, 122-123
Directly visible costs, 71
Dividends, 101-102
Divisions, eliminating need, 95
Duplication among departments, 89

E
Employees
  Appraisal of, 92-93
  Approval to add, 90
  Communication of goals to, 79
  Cross-training of, 92
Equipment
  Availability, 130-131
  Leasing vs. purchase, 110
  Material handling, 134
  Obsolete, 126
  Review of, 144
  Utilization, 129-130
Evaluating operations, 71-97
Evaluation categories, 75-76

F
Favoritism, 93
Financial information, 79-83
Financial reporting systems, 79-83
Fixed assets
  Condition of, 110
  Fully depreciated, 109
  Project re-evaluation, 110
  Rent or buy, 110
Forms
  Control program, 163-167
  Purchasing practices, 166-167
  Standardization, 163-165
Freight payments, 102
Function review, 57-58

G

Goals
  Need to set, 79
  Priority of, 85-86
  Understanding, 79
  Unrealistic, 28

I

Ideas, development of, 174-183
Idea-starter words, 181-182
Imbalanced workloads, 86-87
Importance of costs, 21-24
Incentive rates, shipping, 136
Indirect materials, 142-143
Indirectly visible costs, 71-72
Information
  Financial, 79-83
  Other, 95-96
  Product costs, 125
  Timeliness, 96
Inventories
  ABC Method, 108
  Categories of, 108
  Records, 107
  Seasonal fluctuations, 105
  Slow moving & obsolete, 105-107
Investigating mistakes, 90

L

Labor, direct
  Simplified measuring, 121-122
  Standards, 120-121
  Working smarter, 122-123
Labor, indirect, 140-142
Labor variances, 115

M

Machines (See Equipment)
Mail Room
  Equipment, 160
  Operations, 159-160
Maintenance
  Preventative, 144
  Project control, 143-144
Management
  Consultants, 59
  Support, 88

Manager attitudes, 27-29
Manuals, procedure
  Need for, 83
  Periodic updating, 84-85
Manufacturing methods review
  of, 126
Manufacturing operations
  Necessity of, 135
  Questions to ask, 125-138
Manufacturing overhead, 123-124
Mistakes, investigation of, 90
Material
  ABC Method, 118-119
  Team approach, 119
Material handling
  Cost improvements in, 133-135
  Equipment, 134
Material variances, 114

O

Objectives, formal vs. implied, 54-55
Office supplies
  Centralized purchases, 161-162
  Physical control, 162
  Requisitioning, 162-163
  Standardizing, 160-161
Operations
  Analyzing & understanding, 47-49
Organization
  Design, 95
  Review, 50-51
Order processing, 104
Other current assets, 109
Overhead variances, 115
Overtime, cost of, 142

P

"Passing the Buck," 91
Payment, of freight charges, 102
Planning time, 91-92
Plant location review, 126
Policing
  Activities, 76
  Effort utilized, 89
Postage costs, 157-159
Printing, 166-167
Priority groups, 86

Procedure manuals
  Need for, 83
  Updating system, 84-85
Product costs, evaluating, 113-145
Production runs, Optimum, 131-132
Production schedules
  Based on forecasts, 127-128
  Comparing to actual, 132
  Influences, 128-129
  Who determines, 127
Productive activities, 75
Program review, 67
Project type activities, 74
Purchasing
  Forms, 166-167
  Office supplies, 161-162
Purposes of accounting systems,
  81-83

Q

Questions to ask
  Accounts receivable, 102-105
  Cash, 99-102
  Computers, 168-169
  Fixed assets, 109-110
  General, 73, 79-97
  Inventories, 105-108
  Manufacturing operations, 125-138
  Other current assets, 109
  Shipping department, 136-138

R

Rate classifications, 137
Recognition, 186-187
Records
  Inventory, 107
  of Maintenance costs, 144
Rewards
  for cost improvement ideas, 186-
  187
Routine operations, 74
Reviews
  Cost management, 49
  Employee, 92-93
  Function, 57-58
  Manufacturing methods, 126
  Organization, 50-51

Program, 67-68
Staffing, 58-66

S

Salaries, 139-140
Schedules, production, 127-129
Shift overlap, 129-130
Shipments, consolidation of, 136
Shipping
  Competitive bidding, 136
  Questions to ask, 136-138
  Schedules, 137
Six-Step Cost Management
  Approach, 41-42
  Step One — Review, 44-45
  Step Two, 47-69
  Step Three, 71-97
  Step Four, 171-184
  Steps Five and Six, 185-187
Small orders, freight charges, 138
Staffing
  Approvals required, 90
  Comparisons, 88-90
  Review, 58-59
  Review example, 59-67
Standard cost
  Breakdowns, 116
  Number of, 115-116
  Questions, 115-117
  Systems, 114
  Variances, 114-115
Standardization
  Office forms, 163-167
  Office supplies, 160-161
Storage of office supplies, 162
Subcontracting, 141
Suggestion systems, 88-89
Supervisors
  Attitudes, 186
  Participation, 94, 186
Supplies
  Controlling cost of, 160-163
  Mailing of, 157
Support activities, 75-76

Survey
  of Office supplies, 160-161
  of Forms in use, 163-165
Systems review, 55-57

T

Telephones
  Basic equipment charge, 148-151
  Evaluation assistance, 156-157
  Foreign exchange service, 156
Long distance & message unit
    charges, 151-154
WATS, 154-156
Thinking small, 77
Time
  Developing ideas, 172-173
  Planning, 91-92

U

Unnecessary activities, 76

V

Variable costs, 124
Variances
  Labor, 115
  Material, 114
  Overhead, 115

W

Why
  Businesses fail, 16
  Costs get out of control, 24-27
  Customers buy, 22
  Managers are promoted, 15
Work
  Flow, 132-133
  Load, 92
  Load balance, 86-87
  Order system maintenance, 143-144

X

XYZ Company, examples
  Staffing review, 61-67
  Telephone equipment changes, 149-151
  Understanding of objectives, 51-54

Z

Zero
  Balance accounts, 100-101
  Base budgeting, 67